THE ART OF SAYING NO

HOW TO STAND YOUR GROUND, RECLAIM
YOUR TIME AND ENERGY, AND REFUSE TO BE
TAKEN FOR GRANTED (WITHOUT FEELING
GUILTY!)

DAMON ZAHARIADES

ARTOFPRODUCTIVITY.COM

CONTENTS

OTHER BOOKS BY DAMON ZAHARIADES

The Joy Of Imperfection: A Stress-Free Guide To Silencing Your Inner Critic, Conquering Perfectionism, and Becoming The Best Version Of Yourself!

Is perfectionism causing you to feel stressed, irritated, and chronically unhappy? Here's how to silence your inner critic, embrace imperfection, and live without fear!

The Procrastination Cure: 21 Proven Tactics For Conquering Your Inner Procrastinator, Mastering Your Time, And Boosting Your Productivity!

Do you struggle with procrastination? Discover how to take quick action, make fast decisions, and finally overcome your inner procrastinator!

Morning Makeover: How To Boost Your Productivity,

Explode Your Energy, and Create An Extraordinary Life - One Morning At A Time!

Would you like to start each day on the right foot? Here's how to create quality morning routines that set you up for more daily success!

≈

Fast Focus: A Quick-Start Guide To Mastering Your Attention, Ignoring Distractions, And Getting More Done In Less Time!

Are you constantly distracted? Does your mind wander after just a few minutes? Learn how to develop laser-sharp focus!

≈

Small Habits Revolution: 10 Steps To Transforming Your Life Through The Power Of Mini Habits!

Got 5 minutes a day? Use this simple, effective plan for creating any new habit you desire!

≈

To-Do List Formula: A Stress-Free Guide To Creating To-Do Lists That Work!

Finally! A step-by-step system for creating to-do lists that'll actually help you to get things done!

~

The 30-Day Productivity Plan: Break The 30 Bad Habits That Are Sabotaging Your Time Management - One Day At A Time!

Need a daily action plan to boost your productivity? This 30-day guide is the solution to your time management woes!

~

The Time Chunking Method: A 10-Step Action Plan For Increasing Your Productivity

It's one of the most popular time management strategies used today. Double your productivity with this easy 10-step system.

~

Digital Detox: The Ultimate Guide To Beating Technology Addiction, Cultivating Mindfulness, and Enjoying More Creativity, Inspiration, And Balance In Your Life!

Are you addicted to Facebook and Instagram? Are you obsessed with your phone? Use this simple, step-by-step plan to take a technology vacation!

For a complete list, please visit

http://artofproductivity.com/my-books/

YOUR FREE GIFT

~

I'd like to give you a gift as my way of saying thanks for purchasing this book. It's my 40-page PDF action guide titled *Catapult Your Productivity! The Top 10 Habits You Must Develop To Get More Things Done.*

It's short enough to read quickly, but meaty enough to offer actionable advice that can make a real difference in your life.

You can get immediate access to *Catapult Your Productivity* by clicking the link below and joining my mailing list:

http://artofproductivity.com/free-gift/

In the following pages, I'm going to teach you how to say no with confidence and without guilt. Along the way, you'll develop the assertiveness you need to turn down requests if they fail to align with your goals, needs, and convictions.

NOTABLE QUOTABLES ABOUT SAYING NO

~

66 If you don't prioritize your life, someone else will.
   - Greg McKeown

66 A 'no' uttered from the deepest conviction is better than a 'yes' merely uttered to please, or worse, to avoid trouble.
   - Mahatma Gandhi

66 The difference between successful people and very successful people is that very successful people say 'no' to almost everything."
   - Warren Buffett

PART I

THE PEOPLE-PLEASING HABIT

Think of a friend or acquaintance whom you'd consider to be a typical people pleaser. This individual is probably one of the nicest people you know. He or she is always ready to lend a hand. You can count on him or her to help you whenever the need arises. This person will gladly abandon his or her personal pursuits to cater to *your* wants and needs.

Does this behavior sound disturbingly familiar to you in a personal way? Do you notice aspects of it in yourself? For example, when someone requests your help, do you immediately set aside whatever you're working on and say *"Sure!"*?

And here's the bigger issue: do you regularly feel unhappy, stressed, and exhausted as a result of constantly putting other people's priorities ahead of your own?

If so, this book is for you.

Saying no to people is one of the most important skills you can develop. It frees you to pursue your own interests, both personal and professional. To that end, it'll boost your productivity, improve your relationships, and fill you with a sense of confident calm that may seem alien to you at this moment.

The ability to say no is liberating. But developing the skill is often difficult. For most of us, it requires undoing years of practice to the contrary. For *some* of us, learning to say no counteracts a lifetime of indoctrination from our parents, teachers, bosses, coworkers, and family members.

But it's worth the effort. Once you possess the ability to say no with confidence and grace, and do so with regularity, you'll notice changes in how others perceive you. They'll have more respect for you; they'll place a greater value on your time; and they'll come to see you as a leader rather than a follower.

And that's just the tip of the iceberg.

Interested to know more? Are you ready to finally curb your inclination to please people by saying yes all the time? If so, let me describe my personal experience with being an unabashed people pleaser...

MY PAST LIFE AS A PEOPLE PLEASER

∿

I'm a recovering people pleaser. If you had known me in my high school and college days, you needn't have ever wanted for help. I was there for you. All you had to do was ask. I'd happily sacrifice my own pursuits to help you pursue your own.

This tendency to say yes regardless of my personal circumstances was borne of several factors. We'll cover them in *Part II: Reasons We Struggle To Say No*. For now, it's enough to say that I was the quintessential people pleaser.

And I was miserable.

Every time I said yes to someone, it felt like I was doing the right thing. I was making the other person happy. So how could such a decision be regrettable?

But a little voice would always opine that saying yes to

others was, in effect, saying no to myself. The time given would no longer be available to spend toward my own pursuits. The money given would no longer be available to finance my own needs and interests.

And sure enough, I allowed others to use my time, money, and even my labor toward *their* interests while my interests were placed on the back burner.

For example, I owned a pickup truck while attending college. That made me a prime candidate for helping my friends move. As you might expect, I was regularly asked to do so.

Being a diehard people pleaser, I was quick to say yes. But it was always in opposition to the small voice in my head berating me for putting my own interests and priorities on hold. Worse, this voice was persistent. And it slowly caused me to become resentful - of myself as well as the people who routinely requested my help.

It was a downward spiral.

Each time I was asked to do something for someone, I said yes in spite of myself. So ingrained was the habit of catering to others. But with each acquiescence, a feeling of discontent grew inside me, setting the stage for bitterness and despair. Time and again, I sacrificed my own interests to help others, knowing that doing so was making me increasingly unhappy.

I had no one to blame but myself.

At some point, I decided that I had had enough. I began to reject all requests to help friends move. In fact, I turned down nearly all requests for help of any kind.

In retrospect, I regret taking this approach. It was a knee-jerk reaction spurred by my growing resentment and self-loathing, and too severe in its making. It took me years of experimentation and practice to learn to say no with more grace and thoughtfulness.

The Art Of Saying NO will help you make the transition from always pleasing others to prioritizing your own needs and desires. And importantly, I'll show you how to do it without taking the regrettable hardline approach I used long ago.

THE IMPORTANCE OF PRIORITIZING
YOUR NEEDS

❧

One of the most valuable lessons I've learned is that no one will protect my time or prioritize my needs as vigilantly as me. That's understandable. Most people act out of self-interest; they naturally put their own priorities ahead of others' priorities. But it means each of us is responsible for making sure our personal needs are met.

No one is going to do it for us.

Moreover, it's important that we attend to our own needs *before* attending to the needs of others. This assertion may make you feel uncomfortable, particularly if you strive to be loving and giving in all that you do. But allowing your needs to remain unaddressed while you continuously cater to others is the path toward resentment and bitterness. It can even become a health issue if you run yourself ragged (I speak from experience).

When I advise prioritizing your needs over the needs of others, I'm not suggesting you ignore the latter. Not at all! You can still be there for friends, family members, coworkers, and even strangers, and help them when asked. The important thing is that you avoid abandoning your own priorities in the process. After all, how much use will you be to others over the long run if you don't first attend to yourself?

For example, suppose you agree to help people so often that you begin to skip meals, sacrifice sleep, and forsake activities you enjoy. You'll gradually become so exhausted, irritable, and unhappy that you won't be able or willing to help others.

This is the reason I recommend attending to your needs *first*. Doing so gives you the freedom to attend to other people's needs when you have the time, energy, and inclination. You'll be able to decide to help on a case-by-case basis without risking or forfeiting your own health and happiness.

Consider how flight attendants explain airline safety to passengers. In the event the cabin decompresses, you're supposed to put on *your* oxygen mask before helping others put on *their* masks. Help yourself first. Then, assist others. These instructions aren't intended to promote self-preservation. Rather, the airline knows that if you help others first, you risk succumbing to hypoxia. And that would prevent you from helping *anyone.*

When you prioritize your needs over the needs of others, some folks will persist in their attempts to recruit you to their ends. They won't take no for an answer.

In such cases, you'll need to be assertive…

THE PSYCHOLOGY OF ASSERTIVENESS

～

Many people think assertiveness is something you're born with. But that's incorrect. Assertiveness is a learned trait. In the context of this book, it's a learned *skill*.

Being assertive means having the self-confidence to express your needs and wants, and pursue your own ends, even in the face of opposition. It involves telling people where you stand on a given topic and leaving no room for confusion.

Assertiveness is declaring your point of view and not feeling as if you need others' approval or validation.

For example, suppose you're discussing politics with a friend. Being assertive means expressing your position even if it contradicts your friend's position.

Another example: suppose you're watching the latest blockbuster movie at your local theater, and the person next to you is talking loudly on her phone. Assertiveness is asking her to lower her voice or turn her phone off.

Or suppose a friend asks you to take him to the airport on Friday. If you made other commitments, being assertive means telling him no, even if doing so causes him to react poorly.

At its most basic form, assertiveness is candid communication. Nothing more. That's good news because it means assertiveness isn't a skill you're born with. You can develop it with training and practice.

In *The Art Of Saying NO*, we'll discuss assertiveness as it applies to turning down requests others make of you. That's the purpose of this book. But along the way, you'll find that this single, crucial skill (i.e. saying no) can serve as the launching pad for becoming more assertive in every area of your life.

As you learn to be more assertive, your mindset will change. You'll become more willing to share your ideas with others. You'll be more inclined to ask for things you need and want. You'll be less hesitant to express your opinions, and more ready to speak up for those who are unable or unwilling to speak up for themselves.

And of course, you'll become better and more adept at giving voice to that simple, beautiful word that can literally change your life: "no."

ASSERTIVENESS VERSUS AGGRESSIVENESS

∼

I t's important that we distinguish between being assertive and being aggressive. They're often confused as being similar. But they're entirely different behaviors.

Healthy assertiveness is respectful. As we noted in the previous section, being assertive is nothing more than confidently communicating your position.

Aggressiveness is belligerent. An aggressive individual communicates in a way that's rude, dismissive, and even threatening.

Here are a few examples of each behavior in various situations.

EXPRESSING DISAGREEMENT:

Assertiveness: Listening to the other person, and then sharing a dissenting opinion after the other person has finished speaking.

Aggressiveness: Interrupting the other person and speaking over him or her.

SHARING IDEAS IN A GROUP SETTING:

Assertiveness: Participating in the group dialogue. Allowing others to share their ideas, and expressing thoughts on those ideas in a respectful manner.

Aggressiveness: Trying to dominate the group dialogue. Speaking over others, and tearing their ideas down without consideration for their feelings.

SEEKING SILENCE IN A MOVIE THEATER:

Assertiveness: Asking the offender to lower his or her voice so you can enjoy the movie.

Aggressiveness: Demanding the offender to lower his or her voice, and even threatening violence for noncompliance.

SEEKING recourse for an improperly-prepared drink at Starbucks:

Assertiveness: Explaining the problem (e.g. too much chocolate syrup in an iced mocha) to the barista, and asking him or her to remake the drink while maintaining eye contact.

Aggressiveness: Berating the barista for the mistake, and demanding that the drink be remade while glaring at him or her.

SAYING no when someone asks for help:

Assertiveness: Being direct in declining the request. Suggesting another person who may be able to help the requestor.

Aggressiveness: Barking "NO!" at the requestor, and dismissing and/or belittling him or her for asking.

YOU GET THE IDEA.

Aggressiveness is often an impulse. An aggressive person responds in a hostile or inconsiderate manner, and often regrets doing so later.

By contrast, assertiveness is planned, thoughtful, and considerate. An assertive person communicates his or her position with clarity while taking the other person's feelings into account.

The aggressive individual is loud, opinionated, and self-absorbed. The assertive individual understands how to express his or her point of view with grace.

SAYING NO WITH GRACE

∾

The *Art Of Saying NO* isn't just about learning how to rebuff requests for your time. Anyone can do *that*. Rather, the goal is to learn how to say no without feeling guilty.

And that means using a bit of grace.

Tell me if this scenario sounds familiar:

You're frazzled. You have a mountain of work in front of you and not enough time to get everything done. Making matters worse, your phone keeps ringing, preventing you from making headway. And the problem is compounded by the fact that people keep stopping by your office to ask you for help.

In short, you're feeling overwhelmed and frustrated.

At that moment, another coworker approaches your office. He wants you to do something for him, unaware of your stress and state of mind.

He's in for a surprise.

You've been saying yes to people all day, and you're sick of it. Worse, you're irritated at yourself for continuously catering to your coworkers' needs while allowing your own to go unattended.

Your coworker reaches your office and asks, *"Can you do me a favor?"*

You glare at him, brow furrowed and teeth gritted, and snarl, *"I don't have time for you right now! Can't you see I'm busy?!"*

Your coworker, speechless with eyes wide, slowly backs out of your office. He manages to mutter, *"Gosh, I'm sorry"* before doing an about face and departing.

You watch him walk away and instantly feel guilty.

In this scenario, you've managed to say no. You've successfully rebuffed your coworker's request for help. But the manner in which you've done so has likely caused hurt feelings, resentment, and other negative emotions that'll haunt you later.

I'm ashamed to say this scenario comes from my own life. Many times, back when I was a people pleaser, I'd become overwhelmed and lose my cool. I'd blow up, taking out my frustration on whoever was unlucky enough to catch me at a bad time.

And I'd always regret it.

The Art Of Saying NO will show you a better way. By the

time you've finished reading this book, you'll have all the tools you need to say no with grace and tact, and importantly, without guilt.

WHAT YOU'LL LEARN IN THE ART OF SAYING NO

~

The *Art Of Saying NO* is organized into four parts. In my opinion, each part is essential. Each one addresses a crucial aspect of learning how to set boundaries and say no with confidence and poise.

Furthermore, each part builds on the one that precedes it. Each adds substance and strength to the foundation laid by the one it follows.

By the time you've finished reading *The Art Of Saying NO*, you'll know two important things. First, you'll know precisely why it's so difficult to decline others' requests. Second, you'll know how to do it without feeling guilty, and in a way that increases the respect others have toward you.

Here's a quick breakdown of what you'll find in *The Art Of Saying NO*:

Part I

We're coming to the end of **Part I**. We've laid the ground-work for the ideas and strategies that follow.

I revealed my past as a people pleaser for two reasons. First, I wanted to describe the frustration I experienced in letting others' needs constantly take priority over my own. I'll bet you can relate to this frustration. Second, I wanted to show you that no matter of how difficult you find saying no *today*, you can learn to do it with confidence. If I can do it, you definitely can, too.

Part I also introduced the idea of assertiveness and distinguished it from aggressiveness. This was done to high-light the importance of saying no with grace and respect.

Part II

If we want to change something about ourselves, it's important that we understand why we commit the offending behavior in the first place. To that end, **Part II** explores the reasons we say yes when we know we should say no.

You'll find that some of the reasons are familiar to you because they reflect your personal motivations. Others may seem strange. Upon further inspection, however, you might discover they too play subtle roles in your ongoing struggle to say no to people.

Our goal in **Part II** is to shine a revealing light on our motivations, subconscious or otherwise, and thereby set a clear path for making a positive change.

Part III

In **Part III**, we'll take a close look at specific strategies you can use to rebuff others' requests without feeling guilty. You'll find that many, if not most, of them are intuitive. Keep in mind, it's often the simplest remedies that are the most effective. They're also the ones we tend to overlook.

The strategies detailed in **Part III** will help you to say no in a manner that inspires trust and respect while mitigating the potential of a hostile reaction. In my opinion, they comprise the best approach for turning down requestors while encouraging their admiration over the long haul.

Part IV: Bonus Material

The challenge with learning new strategies is understanding how to apply them in situations that are unique to your experience. You'll discover that's the case with learning how to say no.

Part IV will show you how to implement the strategies described in **Part III**. You'll learn how to apply them with the various people you encounter during the course of a given day, from your friends and extended family members to your boss and coworkers.

AS YOU CAN SEE, we have a lot to cover. But don't worry. Each section of *The Art Of Saying NO* is tightly written. Each one moves quickly, delivering its core advice in as little time as possible.

In the next section, I'll show you how to make the most of the material you'll find in *The Art Of Saying NO*.

HOW TO GET THE MOST VALUE FROM
THIS BOOK

～

The *Art Of Saying NO* is an instruction manual. That might sound boring, but it's actually a benefit. It means the material is presented in a soup-to-nuts fashion. Nothing is left to chance. No matter where you are in the process of learning to say no, this book has you covered.

Moreover, specific material in the book is easy to find. If you need to refresh your memory about a particular concept or strategy, all you have to do is look through the table of contents. The material is organized in a logical, intuitive manner.

You may be tempted to brecze through this book. It's short, and can be read in a couple hours. But if you truly want to get maximum mileage from it, I recommend a different approach. Read each section, and pause once you've done so. Reflect on the material in the context of your life.

For example, in *Part II: Reasons We Struggle To Say No*, we'll talk about the role of low self-esteem, and how it makes us inclined to please people. After you read that section, stop for a moment and think about whether low self-esteem is a personal challenge. Consider how it affects the way you interact with others. Think about how it's an obstacle to getting your needs met.

Reflecting on the material in this way allows you to take mental notes that are unique to your personal experience. You'll find that the material has greater impact.

When we get to *Part III: 10 Strategies For Saying No (Without Feeling Like A Jerk)*, look for opportunities to apply the advice. Try out each strategy and note its effect. How does the requestor react? How does its use influence his or her perception of you? Also, note the extent to which each strategy helps you to regain control of your time.

That's being an *active* reader. It's the best way to make full use of the material you'll find in the following pages.

Positive Change Starts Today

Before we move on to *Part II: Reasons We Struggle To Say No*, I need you to do something for me. It's a simple thing, but critical if you hope to get maximum value from this book. Here it is:

I need you to make a commitment. Pledge that you'll apply the advice in this book.

It's tempting to read *The Art Of Saying NO,* and file it away without taking action. Please don't do that. Reading and learning is only one part of the formula. The other part - arguably, the most important part - is applying what you learn. That's when habits change and life becomes more rewarding.

If you're ready to commit, let's jump in.

PART II

REASONS WE STRUGGLE TO SAY NO

It's one of the smallest words in the English language. Yet, many of us believe it carries such awesome power that we're afraid to say it. In those instances when we *do* manage to say no, we instinctively downplay our intentions, offering excuses and apologies to the requestor.

Why does this tiny word carry such gravity? Why are we so hesitant to utter it?

This section will highlight and explain the most common reasons we have difficulty telling others "no." You'll no doubt recognize a few of them in your own life. As you'll see in the following pages, I have personal experience with nearly all of them.

Most of us were raised to believe that saying no is rude and egocentric. This belief becomes a significant part of our value system. So we spend our childhoods and much of our adult lives trying to live in a way that reflects an image we consider more honorable and respectable.

The result? We end up saying yes to everyone around us, even as we become increasingly frustrated, embittered, and resentful.

You're about to learn the unhealthy reasons you dread saying no. Recognizing them - some are less obvious than others - is the first step toward freeing yourself from the fallacious belief that saying no is mean, cold-hearted, or selfish.

Let's get started...

WE WANT TO AVOID OFFENDING PEOPLE

~

People often take offense at things that aren't intended to *give* offense. An example is hearing the word "no" after they ask for someone's help.

You can probably recall instances when this has happened to you. Someone asks you for your time, attention, or money, and you respectfully decline the request. The individual's reaction is immediate, and openly displayed on his or her face. A furrowed brow, a deep frown, and tight lips betray hurt feelings and indignation.

The individual takes offense. He or she may even utter *"That's rude."* Understandably, this causes you to feel pangs of guilt. As you watch the requestor walk away, the displeasure evident in his or her body language, you can't help but feel as if you've done something wrong.

But let's logically unpack this scenario.

First, it's important to understand how this type of offense surfaces. It has nothing to do with moral outrage, the acrimony we tend to associate with taking offense. Nor is it a reaction to a perceived wrongdoing or act of villainy. Rather, when offense is taken in these circumstances, it usually stems from the requestor's insecurities. He or she internalizes the word "no" as a personal rejection. It stings, which prompts the reaction.

It took me years to come to this realization. When it finally dawned on me, everything changed.

I realized that as long as I was respectful to the individual asking for my help, I wasn't responsible for any offense taken when I said no. This was a liberating feeling! It freed me from my fears of turning down requests.

Think about someone in your life who takes offense upon hearing the word "no." The next time this person asks you for help, and you're unable to offer it, pay attention to how you feel when you decline his or her request. Do you feel guilty? Do you feel as if you've done something wrong?

Realize there's no reason to feel that way. As long as you're being courteous and candid, you're not responsible for any offense taken by the requestor.

WE WANT TO AVOID DISAPPOINTING PEOPLE

∾

I f you're like me, you hate disappointing people. You cringe when you see a look of sadness following your words or actions. You shudder at the possibility that you may have been the cause. Seeing that look can make you feel as if you've let others down.

It's more than just an intellectual realization. You can feel it in your gut.

This guilt is unwarranted. You're not responsible for causing others disappointment when you say no to them. To fully appreciate this fact, it's important to understand how disappointment occurs.

Disappointment springs from unmet expectations. Recall times in your life when you've experienced this emotion. The trigger was undoubtedly something that failed to meet your presumed outcome.

For example, you might have visited a restaurant after reading rave reviews only to find that you disliked the food and ambiance. Neither met your expectations, and you were thus disappointed.

Another example: perhaps you expected your child to receive straight A's on his or her report card, and were surprised to find B's and C's. You were likely disappointed.

Or let's say you're expecting a promotion at work. When you're passed over for the promotion, you feel let down. Why? Because your expectations were unrealized.

Now, consider how this plays out when you say no to someone. Suppose a coworker asks for your help, but you're already overwhelmed by your own responsibilities. So you rebuff the request.

Your coworker becomes visibly disappointed by your refusal to help. But is his or her disappointment truly your fault? Or did your coworker approach you with unrealistic - and perhaps even unfair - expectations regarding your ability and willingness to offer help?

The latter scenario is almost certainly the case unless you had previously promised to help your coworker. That being true, you cannot be held responsible for his or her disappointment.

When you acknowledge this fact, you'll find it easier to let go of your fear of disappointing people when you say no to them. You'll come to appreciate that their disappointment is neither your fault nor responsibility.

This perspective will give you the courage to stop accommodating every request and invitation that comes your way.

WE WANT TO AVOID SEEMING SELFISH

~

Most of us care how others perceive us. We want to be thought of as good, caring, helpful individuals. To that end, we go out of our way to appear so through our actions.

For example, we hold the door open for people. We smile at, greet, and listen to talkative strangers when waiting in line at the grocery store. And when we're asked to help out with something, we instinctively say yes.

To do anything else would be selfish, right? And we certainly don't want folks to think we're selfish.

This thought process is understandable. But it's also wrongheaded. Worse, it can spur us to make poor decisions regarding how we allocate our time and attention among competing demands.

We have a limited number of hours to play with each day. That means every time we say yes to someone, we're saying no to someone or something else. And every time we say no, we free ourselves to spend that time and attention on another person or interest.

In this light, is it truly selfish to say no? I believe it's not. Let me demonstrate with an example from my own life.

I mentioned earlier that I used to be the go-to person when it came time to help friends move. My pickup truck and inclination to say yes made me the first person folks approached when they needed help. Unfortunately, the time I spent accommodating their needs was time I couldn't spend with my family, on my studies, and on the activities I enjoyed.

In other words, by taking care of others, I was consciously neglecting to take care of myself. I was ignoring my family. I was putting my studies on the back burner. And I was growing increasingly stressed and unhappy because I wasn't able to do the things I relished.

It was a terrible way to live.

Self-care isn't selfish. It's *necessary*. The problem is, if you're constantly saying yes to other people, putting their priorities ahead of your own, you won't have the time or energy to care for yourself. And you'll slowly become irritated, cynical, and miserable.

Again, it's a terrible way to live.

Will some people consider you selfish when you say no to them? Of course. You can't control that. And it's worth noting, you're not responsible for them feeling that way.

The most responsible thing you can do is care for yourself before you cater to others. Doing so often means saying no to their requests and invitations. After all, if you use up your time, energy, and attention on others, you won't have any left over for yourself.

And that's no way to live a rewarding life.

WE DESIRE TO HELP OTHERS

~

T hink back to the last time you helped someone. I'll bet it felt good. Your actions or advice improved that person's day, which was probably a fantastic feeling.

That's why many of us love to help people. Knowing that we've contributed to someone else's happiness is its own heady reward. In fact, it can be addictive. Some of us look for ways to help others, even if doing so means ignoring our own needs and responsibilities.

We become caregivers in search of people to care for. When we're asked for help, we jump at the opportunity.

For many of us, the desire to help stems from an inclination to show others we love them. For example, we help family members or close friends because doing so is the simplest way to show them they matter to us.

For others, the desire to help springs from an impulse to play the role of a "white knight," swooping in to save the day. For example, we stop to help a stranded motorist change his or her flat tire.

For still others, helping someone is a way to compensate for a perceived deficit. The gratitude we receive allows us to forget about traits we dislike about ourselves.

These motivations are understandable. But left unchecked, they can cause us to repeatedly ignore our own needs and priorities.

To be sure, helping others is honorable. But your resources are limited. You only have so much time, money, and attention at your disposal. It's important to be prudent in how you use these resources.

There will always be someone who could benefit from your attention. There will always be people who will gladly accept your help if you offer it. But keep in mind, you're not responsible for solving other people's problems. You're responsible for yourself and those who depend on you (e.g. your immediate family).

That doesn't mean you shouldn't help people. Rather, the best way to help people over the long run is to ensure *your* needs are met first.

In other words, make sure that self-care has a higher priority than *giving* care.

WE STRUGGLE WITH LOW SELF-ESTEEM

∼

Self-esteem is a tricky, slippery thing. Sometimes, we're confident to the point that we feel we can conquer the world. Other times, we feel utterly insecure. We second guess ourselves to the point that we're unable to take any action at all.

These feelings affect how we perceive ourselves. They influence our self-image, and shape our sense of self-worth. Insecurity can make us feel inadequate, and even provoke twinges of shame.

It's important to recognize this effect because it discourages us from saying no to people. Here's how it works:

Burdened with a low self-image, we mistakenly believe our time is worth less than others' time. We wrongly assume our goals and interests are inferior to other people's goals and interests. We perceive our value to the world as somehow less than the value offered by those around us.

Given this reasoning, it's no wonder we're inclined to put others ahead of ourselves. It's understandable that, when we're asked to help, we instinctively say yes when we should really say no given our other responsibilities.

This isn't an easy problem to solve. Many of those who struggle with self-esteem issues have done so for years. Some have done so throughout their lives. Improving their self-image is likely to involve a long process with plenty of bumps along the way.

The good news is that saying no can actually improve your sense of self-worth. The more you do it, the more you'll come to realize that your time, commitments, and aspirations are just as important as those of the requestor.

And that's a meaningful step toward improving your self-esteem.

The Art Of Saying NO isn't intended to address or resolve emotional issues. It's intended to help you become more assertive, and overcome the impulse to please people by saying yes to their requests and invitations. Along the way, you'll find that saying no with purpose and grace will give you the confidence to move forward in a way that's consistent with your convictions.

WE WANT OTHERS TO LIKE US

~

The desire to be liked is universal. We want others to be drawn to us, to trust us, and to feel better for having spent time with us.

This desire is hardwired into our psyches. It's how we build connections with other people. We try to relate to them, and empathize with them, in the hope of being accepted by them.

It's unsurprising that we often say yes when we know we should say no. It's an instinctive response borne of our longing for other people's approval.

Here again, I speak from experience. When I was in high school, I wanted desperately to be liked by my peers. And so, whenever someone asked me for a favor, whether that entailed my time, effort, or money, I jumped at the chance.

I was the ultimate people pleaser. I was incapable of saying no since doing so meant abandoning an opportunity to receive someone's approval.

This is a common weakness. Many people struggle with it even if they refuse to admit as much.* But it's important to recognize this yearning for validation as a trigger for our tendency to say yes. When we're aware of our motivations, we can review them and take steps to realign our decisions with our values.

If you routinely say yes to people so they'll like you, keep reading. I'll show you how to short-circuit this impulse, and reclaim your time, energy, and dignity in the process.

And here's something that should excite you: learning to say no with purpose and poise will actually improve your status in the eyes of your friends, family members, and coworkers. You'll no longer be seen as a doormat. Instead, you'll gain their respect and inspire their trust.

---

* I'm happy to share my own embarrassing stories because they provide examples of personal growth. To that end, if *I* can overcome the people-pleasing habit, you can, too!

WE WANT TO APPEAR VALUABLE

~

Think back to the last time you served as a resource for someone. Maybe this person sought your advice about something. Perhaps he or she asked your opinion. Or maybe this individual approached you for information that would benefit him or her in some way.

It felt good, didn't it? It was nice to be appreciated.

All of us like being perceived as valuable by others. We enjoy feeling relevant and important. It gives us higher status in others' eyes, if only for a short time.

Here's the problem: this feeling can be intoxicating, prompting us to constantly seek opportunities to prove our worth and reinforce the idea that we're valuable. This inclination can spur us to say yes to requests when we should say no.

For example, suppose a coworker asks you to help her with a report, and points out that you're an expert on the material. If appearing valuable is important to you, being identified as an expert will feel momentarily exhilarating. You'll be inclined to reinforce that notion by agreeing to her request, even if doing so means putting your own responsibilities on the back burner.

Or suppose a friend asks you to help him move, pointing out that your aid would be invaluable to him. It feels good to be considered important, and you want your friend to continue thinking you're valuable.

So you agree to help him.

Unfortunately, doing so means committing several hours. That's time that might otherwise be spent doing things that are more consequential to you - for example, spending the day with your spouse and kids.

I don't mean to suggest you should always turn down requests for help. That's neither the purpose nor intent of *The Art Of Saying NO*. Rather, I hope to encourage you to recognize your motivations for putting other people's priorities ahead of your own. Case in point: do you regularly say yes to people just to appear valuable in their eyes?

As I mentioned earlier, helping people is a respectable thing to do. But helping people for the wrong reasons will only reinforce a bad habit that'll eventually cause you to feel bitter and resentful.

I'll show you a better way.

WE FEAR MISSING OUT ON OPPORTUNITIES

~

Have you ever said yes to your boss because you were afraid that saying no would disqualify you for a raise, promotion, or new responsibilities? Have you ever said yes to a friend because you feared saying no would cost you a rewarding life experience?

That's the fear of missing out (**FOMO** for short). It's the anxiety we feel at the prospect of being unable to take advantage of opportunities. And it's a common reason many of us say yes even when we realize saying no would be a better decision.

For example, at the workplace, we take on new projects because we fear that declining them will impede the advancement of our careers.

With our friends, we commit ourselves to activities because we're afraid to miss out on rewarding experiences.

Social media only reinforces this tendency. We're constantly reading Facebook on our phones and tablets, watching others post about their experiences, and chiding ourselves for not having our own to post. We end up saying yes to things just so we don't feel left out.

The curious result is that we start to feel unfocused, frustrated, and unhappy, even as we strive to take advantage of every opportunity. Why? Because we inevitably stretch ourselves too thin pursuing things that are inconsequential to us.

So the problem isn't that we say yes to opportunities. The problem is that we fail to discriminate between the wrong opportunities and the right ones.

Remember, there's only so much time in the day. You can't do everything. That means each time you say yes to something, you tacitly say no to something else.

In pursuing *some* opportunities, you miss out on others.

This is one of the reasons it's important to learn to say no. By declining *some* offers, you allow yourself the freedom to say yes to those that'll prove truly rewarding to you.

This change in habit requires a change in mindset. It entails abandoning your fear of missing out while remaining aware of opportunities that are consistent with your goals and interests.

WE SUCCUMB TO EMOTIONAL BULLYING

~

You'll occasionally run into people who refuse to take no for an answer. They'll go to great lengths to compel you to say yes, including using emotional bullying.

Emotional bullying occurs when one person makes another feel afraid, angry, or self-conscious for the purpose of achieving his or her ends. This is accomplished through a variety of means, including the following:

- yelling
- calling
- swearing
- making threats
- lobbing insults

- humiliation
- ostracization
- making accusations

Emotional bullies use the above tactics to cause their victims to feel guilt, fear, shame, and embarrassment. The idea is that people who experience these negative feelings will acquiesce. They'll surrender, saying yes to the abusers if only to stop the abuse.

Emotional bullies know what they're doing. They realize they're being manipulative. They understand they're being rude and unfair to their victims.

That's important to remember. Why? Because it gives you the freedom to stand up to this type of bullying and point out its shortcomings. It also gives you the self-confidence to remain resolute in saying no when the bully is trying to get you to say yes.

For example, suppose you've declined a coworker's request for help so you'll have enough time to meet your own work-related obligations. Your coworker responds by shouting and swearing at you.

One way to respond is to remind your coworker that shouting and swearing is inappropriate and unprofessional. Moreover, the behavior is unlikely to resolve things in a productive manner. You might even ask the bully to describe the last time shouting and swearing actually worked for him or her.

In other words, take the high road.

Because you're aware that the abuser is knowingly

being manipulative, you'll be less compelled by his or her tactics. You won't feel shamed, fearful, guilty, or embarrassed. Instead, you'll recognize the bully's shouting and swearing as indications of his or her personality flaws.

That'll make it much easier to remain assertive and stand your ground.

WE'RE AVERSE TO CONFLICT

~

Many folks have difficulty saying no because they struggle with conflict anxiety. They loathe confrontation, and will do just about anything to avoid it. For them, saying *yes* is a quick and easy way to quash a potential dust-up.

I relate to this tendency. I was raised to abhor conflict. When the person I was talking to appeared to become frustrated, angry, or even mildly disappointed, I'd immediately try to assuage them. When such feelings were triggered by something I had said, I'd immediately retract my statements.

Here's an example of how such conversations progressed:

Requestor: "Damon, can I ask you a favor?"

Me: "Sure. What do you need?"

Requestor: "Can you take me to the airport this Friday?"

Me: "I'm sorry. I can't do it this Friday."

Requestor (getting angry): "Are you serious? You're not going to help me?"

Me (with a deer-in-the-headlights stare): "Uhh…"

Requestor (getting angrier): "Don't ever ask me for anything in the future!"

Me (desperate to end the conflict): "Okay. Calm down. I'll take you to the airport."

Acquiescing to the requestor's demand was easier than standing my ground. This was the case because I had such a strong resistance to conflict. I was willing to give in just to avoid a confrontation.

Maybe you can relate. Perhaps you tend to say yes to people so they won't be angry or frustrated with you. You've learned that being nice stifles any chance of a showdown.

The problem is, capitulating to avoid conflict reinforces the idea that your feelings are less important than those of the other person. The reality is, they're *not* less important. You're just being made to feel that way.

If you're afraid of conflict, there are small, simple things you can do to overcome that fear. First, recognize that harmony isn't always possible. People have conflicting opinions, needs, and desires. Friction is inevitable.

Second, remind yourself that conflict isn't necessarily

bad. It's merely the expression of contradictory views. How a person reacts to a conflict (with a calm demeanor or with anger) is an entirely different matter.

Third, practice saying no in small steps. Start with situations where confrontations are likely to be nonexistent. An example is telling a salesperson at a clothing store that you don't want to buy an article of clothing.

Gradually introduce situations where saying no is likely to have a larger reaction. An example is telling a used car salesman that you don't want to purchase a vehicle.

By starting with low-risk situations, you'll build a tolerance for conflict. Like a muscle, this tolerance will become stronger with repeated use. You'll eventually grow comfortable saying no, even when faced with someone prone to anger when his or her requests are denied.

WE DEVELOP THE PEOPLE-PLEASING
HABIT

~

S aying yes is an ingrained habit for many of us. It's something we learn to do over a long period of time. The longer we do it, the more entrenched the habit becomes until it's instinctive. We do it on autopilot, agreeing to things before we even realize we're doing so.

In a sense, we've wired our brains to respond in that way whenever people ask things of us.

Think about the last time you agreed to do something you weren't even remotely interested in. Did you find yourself saying yes before you had even considered how doing so might impact you?

That's a learned behavior.

It can stem from a number of factors. For example, you

might have learned as a child that saying yes resulted in approval from your parents or other authority figures. Or you may have found that saying yes made others happy, and that, in turn, gave you a sense of self-worth. Or you might have discovered that saying yes to your peers made them more inclined to include you.

Such "lessons" have a powerful effect on us. They train us to accommodate others as doing so affords us short-term benefits (approval, sense of self-worth, and social inclusion). The more "lessons" we observe, the greater our desire to repeat the outcome.

We become addicts looking for our next "fix."

The good news is that, like any habit, the tendency to instinctively say yes can be unlearned. It can be undone. We can rewire our brains so we're more contemplative about the requests being made of us.

The key, as always, is to take small steps.

For example, in the beginning, just focus on *not* saying yes immediately. Give yourself a few moments to consider requests and how they'll impact your day. Interrupting your instinctive response will help to short circuit the habit.

Next, examine the reasons you're inclined to say yes. Are those reasons valid? For example, do you desire the requestor's approval? Do you need that person to validate your sense of worth? Is it important to you that you're included in his or her circle of friends? You may find that this learned behavior (i.e. automatically saying yes) is prompted by motivations that are trivial to you.

It's not easy to reverse a habit you've developed over years of repeated application. But it *can* be done. The first - and arguably most important - step is to recognize the habit exists.

POP QUIZ: ARE YOU A PEOPLE PLEASER?

~

L et's find out how inclined you are to say yes to people. Most of us struggle with this problem at some level. But there's a huge chasm that separates the *occasional* people pleaser and the *chronic* people pleaser.

It's time to find out where you land on the scale.

Below you'll find 15 statements. Read each one, and assign a value from one to five. Write down "1" if the statement is completely false as it applies to you. Write down "5" if the statement describes you to a T. If a statement is somewhat accurate, assign values "2," "3," or "4" to indicate the extent.

Once you've assigned values to each of the following 15 statements, we're going to tally your score. Your score will reveal how likely you are to abandon your own needs and priorities to accommodate other people.

1. I never speak my mind, even when I have strong feelings about something.
2. I always feel the need to smile and be overly nice to people, even when I'm feeling grumpy.
3. The possibility of conflict terrifies me.
4. I immediately feel selfish when I do something for myself.
5. I regularly allow friends, coworkers, family members, and even strangers, to violate my personal boundaries.
6. I always try to be the person others want me to be.
7. I regularly sacrifice my emotional happiness to make sure other people are happy.
8. I am fearful of others' negative emotions toward me.
9. I desperately want to be liked by others.
10. I avoid taking initiative.
11. Rejection frightens me.
12. I overanalyze every decision, concerned with how my decisions will cause others to react.
13. I soar emotionally when I receive positive feedback and crumble into despair when I receive negative feedback.
14. I'm convinced everybody is good, even when an

individual is abusive and emotionally manipulative toward me.

15. Saying "no" fills me with an immediate sense of dread.

Let's now tally your score to see how likely you are to say yes to people, even at the cost of your own happiness.

15 TO 30 points - You have little difficulty saying no. You make judicious decisions regarding how to use your time and other resources, and remain resolute when others disparage those decisions. Meeting your obligations, addressing your responsibilities, and caring for your own happiness have a higher priority than pleasing people.

31 TO 45 points - You sometimes feel conflicted when pursuing your personal and/or professional goals, knowing you could be helping others realize theirs. Saying no isn't a *major* problem for you, and you often decline requests out of necessity. Nevertheless, you say yes more often than you'd like.

46 TO 60 points - You're driven to please people, even if you're not consciously aware of it. You're highly averse to conflict, and go to great lengths to avoid it. When confronted with another's anger, irritation, distress, or displeasure, you immediately drop what you're doing to rescue that person. Rescuing him or her usually entails surrendering to the individual's requests.

61 TO 75 points - Everything you do, from the moment you wake up, is geared toward making other people happy. You rarely consider your own happiness, and are willing to set aside your own goals and responsibilities to accommodate others. You maintain no personal boundaries, allowing people to intrude upon you at their whim. The idea of saying no is unimaginable since doing so might negatively affect others. You are, in effect, a chronic people pleaser.

IF YOUR SCORE is greater than 30, I have good news. You'll find the tactics and strategies covered in *Part III: 10 Strategies For Saying No (Without Feeling Like A Jerk)* will deliver immediate, practical value.

Fair warning: applying the advice won't be easy. The people-pleasing habit is a difficult one to break. But it *is* possible regardless of how ingrained the habit is in your psyche. The remainder of *The Art Of Saying NO* will guide you step by step toward transforming this aspect of your life.

Coming Up Next

You're aware of the problem, and the degree to which it impacts your daily experience. You also recognize the reasons you put other people's priorities ahead of your own. But you're unsure what to do to break the habit.

I'll show you what to do in *Part III: 10 Strategies For Saying No (Without Feeling Like A Jerk)*. We're going to cover a variety of ways you can turn down requests with grace, poise, and integrity.

Are you ready to vanquish your inner people pleaser? If so, grab a beverage, get comfortable, and read on…

PART III

10 STRATEGIES FOR SAYING NO (WITHOUT FEELING LIKE A JERK)

~

The biggest challenge you face when learning to say no is overcoming the feelings of guilt, fear, and shame that surface when you disappoint people. That's no small task. In many cases, it requires unraveling years of training.

Some of us, myself included, have spent the majority of our lives accommodating others. We've trained ourselves through continuous application to put others before ourselves. Reversing that habit will take a fair amount of time and effort.

The good news is, anybody can do it. If you're willing to apply the tactics I'll share with you in the following pages, you'll gradually curb your people-pleasing tendencies. As you say no more and more often, you'll discover that doing so gives you the freedom to spend your time pursuing more productive and rewarding endeavors.

As I mentioned earlier, this isn't about refusing to help people. Rather, the goal is to learn how to say no without feeling guilty when you know it's the best decision given your circumstances.

With that out of the way, let's jump in and discuss Strategy #1.

STRATEGY #1: BE DIRECT AND STRAIGHTFORWARD

~

Does the following scenario sound familiar?

Someone asks you for help. The problem is, you're swamped with projects, and consequently lack the time to lend a hand. You know you must say no to the person's request. There's no other option given the volume of work on your plate.

But you don't respond with *"I'm sorry. I'm unable to help you."* Instead, you hem and haw, and eventually say *"Ummm... maybe, but I'm kinda busy. I don't know how much time I can spare."*

This sends a mixed message to the requestor. It tells him or her that you're otherwise engaged, but may be receptive to the request. It signals that you might be persuaded to set aside your responsibilities to accommodate him or her.

The requestor is likely to take advantage of the opportunity by conveying a heightened sense of urgency (e.g. *"This is super important, and I really need your help right now!"*).

When you waffle in response to a request, you inadvertently welcome increased pressure from the requestor. The individual asking for your time will take your waffling as a sign of indecision. He or she will recognize that you can be coaxed toward his or her ends, even if that means you risk missing your own deadlines.

For this reason, it's always better to be clear when you decline requests. Don't beat around the bush. Don't equivocate, hoping that it'll pacify the requestor (it won't). Instead, be candid about your unwillingness to consent to his or her request.

Being straightforward when turning down requests doesn't mean you're being discourteous. In fact, your candidness is likely to be appreciated by the requestor, who'll know that trying to persuade your accommodation will be a waste of time. The individual can spend that time more wisely looking elsewhere for assistance.

It helps to have a reason for saying no. Your reason validates your inability and/or unwillingness to lend a hand. For example, consider the following two responses to a request for help…

1. "I don't have time to help you."
2. "I don't have time to help you because I'm

working on a crucial report that's due in
two hours."

The first response prompts the requestor to wonder
whether your refusal to help is a personal rejection. That
can lead to a confrontation, which helps neither party.

The second response eliminates rejection as a possibility. Instead, it justifies your decision as reasoned and practical. The requestor may dislike your decision, but will be
more likely to accept it at face value.

Be honest about your reason for turning down the
requestor. Resist the temptation to make something up.
Not only will you feel guilty for lying, but the requestor is
likely to notice your lack of sincerity. And that may cause
him or her to become resentful toward you.

The best approach is to be direct, honest, and
respectful.

STRATEGY #2: DON'T STALL FOR TIME

~

Y ou can tell when someone is stalling. Likewise, others can tell when *you* do it. None of us are as inconspicuous as we think.

Yet many of us are still tempted to stall for ·time when someone asks us for help. We know we're unable to spare the time and/or energy. We realize the answer must ultimately be no. But instead of giving the requestor a direct response, we beat around the bush and delay the inevitable.

For example, we respond by asking, *"Can I get back to you on that?"* Or we tell the requestor, *"Let me think about it when I have a free moment."*

Sometimes we do it to be tactful. We know we must decline the request, but we don't want the requestor to think we're rejecting him or her. We don't want the individual to think it's personal.

Other times we do it out of fear. We're concerned that refusing to put the requestor's needs before our own will trigger a confrontation. So, we stall in the hopes of lessening the impact of our refusal.

Still other times we delay because we truly want to help the individual, but are swamped and uncertain how to do it. We stall for time, hoping to figure out how to meet our own obligations while accommodating the requestor.

Stalling is a bad idea for a few reasons. First, it strings the requestor along. It encourages him or her to hold out hope for your help even though there's little chance you'll be able to deliver. When the requestor realizes you're unable to offer assistance, and his or her time has been wasted, he or she is likely to become irritated.

Second, stalling makes you appear indecisive. When you fail to respond with a direct "no," the requestor may become more assertive, believing you can be persuaded to acquiesce.

Third, stalling for time reduces your productivity by prolonging the situation. It forces you to spend more time than necessary declining the request.

When someone asks you for help, and you know you must turn down the request, don't stall. Be direct and clear. Doing so may feel uncomfortable. It may even prompt the requestor to respond in anger. But you can't control his or her response nor the emotions behind it.

Being sincere with a direct "no" shows respect. It also

prevents the request from hanging over your head like a dark, ominous cloud.

STRATEGY #3: REPLACE "NO" WITH ANOTHER WORD

~

S aying no can have negative effects, even if you do it with grace. For example, someone asking for your help might be offended if he or she associates the word "no" with a personal rejection. This individual might become angry if his or her ego is hurt by your response.

These reactions can occur regardless of how tactful you are in declining the request. The word "no" carries an air of finality. Many people are ill-prepared to hear it, and lack the ability to accept it with poise and understanding.

After repeatedly interacting with such folks, we learn that saying no to them is not only difficult, but also costly. Oftentimes, these people leave in anger and tell their peers that we're inflexible and unwilling to help. This can burn bridges, jeopardize our reputations, and impact our careers.

Is it any wonder that we have difficulty saying no to people?

The good news is that it's possible to decline requests without saying the word "no." It's just a matter of finding different ways to communicate the same message.

For example, suppose a family member asks you to take him to the airport. You could simply say no and provide a sincere reason. If he's sympathetic to your circumstances, that should suffice.

But let's say you know from past experience that he's *not* sympathetic. He's inclined to hear "no" as a personal rejection, and likely to be angered by it. To avoid this reaction, how else might you decline his request?

Here are a few examples:

66 I can't commit to that right now because I'm focused on a high-priority project."

This response tells the family member that you're busy and unable to break away from your work.

66 I'd like to help you, but I'm swamped with this project right now."

This response lets the family member know that he's important to you, but there's a valid reason you're unable to accommodate him.

" People are depending on me to finish this project. If I abandon it to help you, I'd be letting them down."

This response explains that you're forced to decline the request because of a prior commitment. Most people would hesitate before asking you to desert your obligations.

Notice how none of the above examples use the word "no." It's a difficult word to say because it's a difficult word to *hear*. Turning down requests in ways that allow you to avoid saying no outright can help soften the blow. That can defuse any potential confrontation with the requestor.

This approach can be effective for any type of request. It'll work just as well when you're asked for money as it will when you're asked to devote your time or labor.

STRATEGY #4: RESIST THE URGE TO OFFER EXCUSES

I understand the temptation.

Someone asks you for help. You can't spare the time, so you must turn down the request. But you don't want the individual to think you're blowing him or her off, so you scramble to come up with excuses. For example...

- "I can't take you to the airport because my car's in the shop."
- "I can't help you move tomorrow because I threw out my back."
- "I can't contribute funds for Tom's retirement party because I don't have any cash on me."

- "I can't babysit your kids because I have to stay late at the office."
- "I can't help you build your deck today because I promised my kids I'd take them to the movies."

You get the point.

The excuses are an attempt to deceive the person asking you for help. For example, your car is fine, your back is healthy, you have cash in your wallet or purse, you're planning to leave the office at 5:00 p.m., and your kids haven't a clue you're taking them to the movies.

In other words, you made up the excuses to justify turning down the requests.

There are two problems with this approach. First, you're likely to feel guilty for misleading the requestor. Worse, the requestor will probably be able to recognize your deception. Remember, as I noted in *Strategy #2: Don't Stall For Time*, none of us are as discreet as we imagine. The result is that we risk earning a reputation for being untrustworthy.

Second, it opens the door to negotiations, which require time and effort. For example, suppose your neighbor asks you to help him build his deck this afternoon. You decline the request, explaining that you promised to take your kids to the movies. He responds by saying, *"That's fine. Can you help me tomorrow?"*

Now what will you do? One option is to come up with yet another excuse (e.g. *"I can't help because I have to take my wife to the doctor."*). But that'll make you appear disingenuous.

You've essentially painted yourself into a corner.

The better approach is to turn down the request with a simple no, and resist the temptation to say more. This needn't come across as rude or mean. On the contrary, as long as you're civil, being direct shows respect.

As a bonus, doing this consistently increases your self-confidence. That'll make it easier for you to gracefully decline requests in the future.

STRATEGY #5: TAKE OWNERSHIP OF YOUR DECISION

∽

Have you ever noticed how easy it is to say "I can't" when someone asks for your time, money, or labor? For some of us, the response is practically automatic. It's a reflex. We say "I can't" before we're able to consider what it means.

In most cases, we actually *can* help. It's technically possible for us to do so. We can surrender our time. We can give money. And notwithstanding physical ailments, we can offer our labor. But when we turn down requests, we choose to say *"I can't."*

This response allows us to avoid taking ownership of our decisions. We get into the habit of turning people down without expressing our decisions as a matter of personal choice.

In my opinion, this has a harmful effect over the long run. If we avoid taking ownership of our decisions to decline requests, we never feel truly empowered with a sense of personal agency. Every time we say "I can't," we train our minds to avoid taking responsibility. "I can't" implies that we're at the mercy of external constraints.

Over time, this gives us the false sense that we're not in control. We begin to believe that external factors undermine our authority - that our personal decisions aren't truly our own to make.

That's the opposite of empowering. It's *disempowering*. And it can have a significant negative psychological effect on our behaviors and thoughts.

The good news is that there's a simple, if not easy, solution. When you must turn down a request or invitation, express your decision as a personal choice. Instead of telling the requestor, "*I can't*," tell him or her:

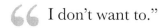 I don't want to."

Give a reason if you suspect doing so will defuse a potentially combative response. (Make sure your reason is sincere and not simply an excuse.) The important thing is that you *own* your decision.

Responding in this manner to requests you're unable to accommodate is an affirmation of your will and personal authority. You're not blaming external constraints for your refusal to help. You're making conscious choices regarding how you spend your time, energy, and other limited resources.

The more you use phrasing that expresses your will, the more confident you'll become in turning down requests that conflict with your needs and convictions. And the more respect you'll inspire in those who seek your help.

STRATEGY #6: ASK THE REQUESTOR TO FOLLOW UP LATER

∼

This isn't a stalling tactic. Rather, it's a way to revisit a request when you have more time to think about it. It also allows you to put the onus on the requestor while gauging the urgency of his or her request.

For example, let's say a harried coworker bursts into your office and exclaims, "*I really need your help on this project.*" Because you're busy with your own tasks, you're unable to accommodate him at that moment. But you might be able to lend a hand later, after you've completed your work.

To that end, you respond:

66 I don't have time to help you right now. But

check in with me after 4:00 p.m. Things will be less crazy then."

With this response, you eliminate all of the pressure placed on you by the requestor. You're able to address your own responsibilities without having to think about whether the request is something you want to take on. You can revisit it later, and make your final decision, even if you ultimately decide that you don't want to help.

It also conveys your willingness to at least consider his or her request. You're not rejecting him or her, or dismissing the request outright. On the contrary, you're showing that you care, you're interested, and may be willing to lend a hand.

Note that you're not obligating yourself to say yes when the requestor follows up. You may want to emphasize this fact, if only to temper his or her expectations.

Oftentimes, you'll find taking this approach leads to one of two outcomes. The first possible outcome is that the requestor seeks help elsewhere. That's great for everyone involved. You're able to continue working without abandoning your own tasks. Meanwhile, the requestor receives the assistance he or she needs in a more timely manner.

The second possible outcome is that the requestor decides to complete his or her project *without* help. The individual realizes he or she possesses the necessary expertise, and finds the confidence to move forward on his or her own.

Of course, if the individual *does* follow up with you, you can decide at that time whether saying yes is a good idea. By then, you'll have considered the request, and reflected upon whether - and to what extent - lending a hand might negatively impact your own goals.

STRATEGY #7: AVOID LYING ABOUT YOUR AVAILABILITY

~

I understand the temptation. Someone asks you to do something you'd rather avoid. As an honest person, you'd like to tell them as much. The problem is, you fear that honesty is likely to cause him or her to feel offended, upset, or resentful.

So you lie.

For example, you tell the requestor, "*Sorry. I can't take you to the airport because I have a doctor's appointment.*" In truth, you have no plans to visit your doctor. The excuse is just a way to get out of accommodating the request.

It's a small, harmless lie. You tell yourself that it's not as if you're hurting someone. There are far worse sins than lying about your availability.

But it carries consequences. When you tell these small,

harmless lies, you erode your sense of personal authority. You train yourself to fear what others might think about your reasoning.

For example, suppose the real reason you're turning down the requestor is that you simply dislike driving to the airport. Additionally, you want to avoid becoming known as the "taxi" person - the one to whom everyone turns when they need a lift.

Here's how you might express these feelings when someone asks you to take him or her to the airport.

> I don't want to drive to the airport because I can't stand freeway traffic."

> I don't want to drive to the airport because the ride, up and back, will take three hours."

> I've had a terrible week and had planned to relax today. So I'm going to say no."

> I'm going to pass. I don't want to be the one everyone asks to take them to the airport."

On the surface, these responses might seem impolite. On the contrary, you're being direct, which shows respect. You're showing the requestor that you hold him or her in high enough regard to be candid. You trust that he or she will respect your feelings, and honor your wishes on the matter.

But most importantly, you train yourself to trust your own authority. Rather than lying about your availability and feeling guilty for doing so, you develop a strong sense of personal agency. You learn to rely on your own reasoning when deciding whether to consent to, or turn down, requests and invitations.

As you develop and strengthen this confidence and resoluteness, you'll become less concerned with how the requestor reacts to your saying no. You'll recognize that as long as you decline requests with grace, honesty, and respect, the requestor's reaction isn't your responsibility.

STRATEGY #8: OFFER AN ALTERNATIVE

～

No one likes to be left hanging. When you say no, give the requestor another option. It'll go a long way toward mitigating his or her disappointment at your inability or unwillingness to lend a hand.

For example, suppose John, a coworker, drops by your office and asks you to help him with a project. You're busy with your own work-related responsibilities, and therefore plan to turn him down. But rather than leaving him hanging with a simple "no," you'd like to give him another option.

Options usually come in the form of mentioning others who might be able to help in your stead. For example:

66 I'm going to pass, John. But you might ask

Tony. I know he has some downtime, and may be able to help you."

❝ I want to help, but I'm swamped until 4:00 p.m. If this can't wait, hit up Shelley. She may be available to help you right now."

❝ Your project sounds complex, John. I'm focused on my own tasks, and don't want to break away from them and lose my momentum. But I know Mark and Sandra are looking for a challenge to sink their teeth into."

If you're currently helping the requestor with another task or project, options can also take the form of an either-or decision. For example:

❝ John, I'm barely keeping my head above water helping you with Project ABC. I can continue to help you with that one or help you with this new one. But not both. Which one would you prefer me to work on?"

If helping the requestor requires handling multiple tasks, offer to handle a smaller number as an alternative. For example:

❝ John, I want to help, but I don't have time to create the PowerPoint presentation, train the subject matter experts, and manage the test team. But I'm happy to do the PowerPoint presentation for you. Fair enough?"

This approach doesn't only work in an office environment. It works with friends, family members, neighbors, and even strangers. By offering the requestor an alternative, you're showing him or her that you care. You're also lessening the requestor's disappointment at hearing you turn down his or her request.

Keep in mind, you don't owe the requestor alternatives. It's just an act of goodwill. Nothing more. But there's a good chance the alternative you offer, whether it's to refer the requestor to someone else or offer a lesser degree of help, will be met with appreciation.

STRATEGY #9: SUGGEST ANOTHER PERSON WHO'S BETTER QUALIFIED

~

You'll sometimes receive requests that are better handled by other people. Declining these requests is good for all parties. You're able to save time, and can focus on your own projects and interests; the requestor receives the specialized help he or she needs; and the person to whom you refer the requestor will have an opportunity to show his or her proficiency.

There are many reasons to refer requestors to other people. For example, you might do so because you know someone who has more experience than you in the matter.

Suppose your friend Joan, a novelist, asks you to critique her latest manuscript. Doing a full critique takes more than just time; it requires paying close attention to pacing, dialogue, point-of-view consistency, and other story elements. This is an opportunity to refer Joan to someone who's more qualified. For instance, you might tell her:

> Joan, because I've never critiqued a manuscript, I'd rather not critique yours. It's not an area of strength for me. But my friend Susan does this sort of thing for fun. I'll bet she'd be happy to help."

Notice that you're not simply saying no and leaving Joan hanging. Although you're turning down her request, you're helping her by referring her to a qualified, and potentially valuable, resource.

Here's another example: suppose you're a manager and your coworker Stephen asks you to review his financial analysis on a particular project. You're not an expert on the subject. But lucky for Stephen, you know someone who is. You might respond as follows:

> I don't want to take this on because I have a poor grasp of the financial side of things. But Toby in accounting is a crack shot with this stuff. Ask him to look over your analysis. Tell him I sent you."

Again, you're not leaving Stephen hanging without options. You're pointing him toward someone who's better able to help him. And you're smoothing the introduction by telling him to mention your name to Toby.

Sometimes, it makes sense to refer the requestor to someone else who's working on a similar project or has similar interests.

For example, suppose your cousin - let's call him Franklin - asks you to go golfing with him. You have no interest in golf, and therefore want to decline the invitation. But rather than leave your cousin hanging, you mention your mutual friend Tom, who loves to golf. You might say the following to Franklin:

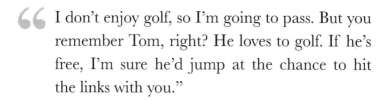 I don't enjoy golf, so I'm going to pass. But you remember Tom, right? He loves to golf. If he's free, I'm sure he'd jump at the chance to hit the links with you."

By referring the requestor to someone else - notably, someone who's better qualified than you or shares an interest with the requestor - you're helping even though you're declining his or her request. It's a great way to say no without feeling guilty. And by pointing the requestor to a more suitable partner or resource, you're doing him or her a favor.

STRATEGY #10: DESCRIBE YOUR LACK OF BANDWIDTH

◁∾▷

T his is one of my favorite ways to say no. It leaves the requestor with no room to pressure me into accommodating his or her request.

Here's how it works:

Suppose your to-do list is filled with tasks and projects that'll take up most of your day. You know this ahead of time because you're adept at estimating the amount of time you'll need to complete various tasks.

Now, suppose your friend asks you to help him move. You suspect the move will take at least three hours. There's no way you can fit the job in given your to-do list. You must turn down your friend's request.

One way to do that is to simply say *"I don't have enough time to help you move."* But that's likely to prompt your friend to try to negotiate: *"C'mon, it'll only take an hour. You can spare an hour, can't you?"*

You might rightfully respond, *"An hour?! It'll take at least three hours."*

At that point, your friend might counter, *"Tell you what. Help me for the first hour and then you can leave."*

And on and on it goes, back and forth.

You can short circuit this process by describing your day to your friend and explaining why you don't have enough time to help. For example, you might say:

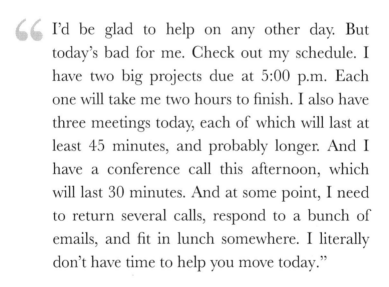 I'd be glad to help on any other day. But today's bad for me. Check out my schedule. I have two big projects due at 5:00 p.m. Each one will take me two hours to finish. I also have three meetings today, each of which will last at least 45 minutes, and probably longer. And I have a conference call this afternoon, which will last 30 minutes. And at some point, I need to return several calls, respond to a bunch of emails, and fit in lunch somewhere. I literally don't have time to help you move today."

For this approach to be effective and guilt-free, you actually need to have a busy day ahead of you. In other words, don't just make things up to *appear* busy.

By describing your lack of bandwidth in detail, you're letting the requestor know that you have other responsibilities. Abandoning these responsibilities isn't an option for you. Meanwhile, the requestor doesn't feel as if you're rejecting him or her. On the contrary, it becomes clear that you sincerely are unavailable to lend a hand.

Few requestors will try to negotiate with you or compel you to help once they understand what's on your plate.

BONUS STRATEGY #1: BE RESOLUTE

~

You'll inevitably encounter people who will refuse to take no for an answer. They'll persist when you turn down their requests. They'll attempt to cajole you into accepting their invitations. They might use emotional manipulation or even outright intimidation to compel you to accommodate them.

First, realize that you can't control how others behave. If someone persists after you've turned him or her down, remind yourself that the individual's persistence has nothing to do with the validity of your choices. Some people are simply pushy.

Second, the moment you second guess your decision, a pushy requestor is likely to notice and become more persistent. He or she will see an opening and be inclined to take advantage of it.

For these reasons, if you decide to turn down a request, it's important to remain unswerving in that decision. Assuming you made the decision for the right reasons, there's no cause to doubt yourself.

One way to stand your ground when the requestor becomes pushy is to acknowledge his or her pushiness. For example, you might say:

> Sharon, I know you dislike hearing no, and are inclined to persist. But I'm not going to change my mind."

Another tactic is to ask pointed questions that force the requestor to justify his or her request of you. For example, you might ask:

> Who else have you asked for help?"

Or:

> Given my lack of expertise, I'm not the best person to ask for help with this task. Did you already ask Carl or Janet, our resident experts?"

Sometimes, a requestor will persist, even after you've

made it clear that you're turning down his or her request and intend to remain resolute. The individual may try to negotiate with you. He or she may even demand a reason for your refusal to help.

In such cases, it's fine to be more assertive. Don't be afraid to push back. For example, you might respond:

> Listen Sam. I'll save you some time. I'm not going to help you with this project. And I can guarantee you that I'm not going to change my mind."

You shouldn't feel guilty about responding in this manner. It's not rude at all. You're simply being direct, telling the requestor that his or her efforts to compel you to backtrack on your decision are wasted.

It's possible that the requestor will be taken aback by your directness. Note that this response isn't a reflection of whether your decision is appropriate. It's merely a reaction, and one over which you have no control.

There's a bonus benefit to staying resolute when you turn down requests. When you do it consistently, people will gradually realize that you can't be manipulated, intimidated, or otherwise pressured to change your mind.

BONUS STRATEGY #2: BE COURTEOUS

~

I t's difficult to remain polite when a requestor becomes rude and demanding. It's tempting to respond in kind, if only to show him or her that you're not a pushover. It's tough to suppress that impulse.

But it's also crucial if you want to manage how others perceive you. Respond in an uncivil manner, and you might hurt your career or harm the relationships you share with others.

For example, suppose you respond impolitely to a coworker who has asked you for your help. He or she might consider you unprofessional and share that perspective with others in your office.

Suppose a family member invites you to a party, and you decline with a snide remark. At the very least, his or her feelings are likely to be hurt. You can also assume he or she will share your response (with embellishments) to other family members.

Let's say a friend asks you to help him move. You dislike such requests because they make you feel taken for granted. You respond in frustration, turning down your friend in a rude, disrespectful way. Doing so is sure to impact your friendship (at least, until you apologize).

You can be assertive and courteous at the same time. The former informs the requestor that you're confident in your decisions. The latter shows him or her respect, which lessens the likelihood of a hostile response.

Additionally, being courteous shows that you're in control of yourself. You're not prone to enraged outbursts. Instead, you maintain a businesslike professionalism that's difficult to fault. For example, you might say:

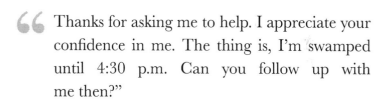 Thanks for asking me to help. I appreciate your confidence in me. The thing is, I'm swamped until 4:30 p.m. Can you follow up with me then?"

This approach reduces tension, and thereby quashes the likelihood of a bitter reaction. By expressing your appreciation, you're showing grace. By asking the requestor to follow up with you at a later time, one during which you're available, you're showing him or her a willingness to help, if only on your terms.

When you say no to someone, courtesy and assertiveness work hand in hand. You'll find that being courteous will encourage people to perceive you as respectful, compassionate, and attentive. These traits, in turn, will encourage them to accept your "no" at face value.

BONUS STRATEGY #3: CONFRONT YOUR FEAR OF MISSING OUT

∼

The fear of missing out (FOMO) motivates many of us to say yes, even when we lack the time, energy, or money to do so with confidence. We cringe at the mere possibility that we might let an opportunity slip through our fingers. So we say yes when we know we should say no.

For example, we accept an invitation to a party just in case someone we want to meet is in attendance. The chance that this person will show up is small, but we don't want to miss out in the event he or she does.

Or we agree to take on a big project at the office because doing so *might* lead to a promotion down the road. In reality, the odds that it'll do so are tiny. But we say yes because we don't want to miss out if there's the slightest chance.

According to psychologists, the fear of missing out is serious enough to induce anxiety in many people. It can even be the cause of compulsive behavior, such as checking email and Facebook messages every few minutes.

Most of us struggle with FOMO to some extent. The important thing is to recognize its role in prompting us to say yes without first considering whether doing so is a good idea.

For example, suppose you have an opportunity to manage a new project at your job. You're inclined to say yes because there's a chance that taking it on might advance your career.

But there are probably concealed costs associated with managing this project. For example, saying yes to *this* project means you must say no to others, some of which might offer better odds of career advancement.

Also, consider your availability given what's already on your plate. Do you have enough time to take on another project? If not, taking it on is likely to have a negative impact on your current responsibilities. Falling behind and turning in shoddy work is more likely to *hurt* your career than help it.

Take stock of whether the fear of missing out is spurring you to say yes when you're better off saying no. If it is, you must train yourself to control it.

It'll take time and patience, and perhaps even a bit of courage. The next time you instinctively want to say yes to an offer, request, or invitation, stop. Take a moment to think it through. Are you willing to say yes because there's a high likelihood that doing so will pay dividends? Or are you saying yes simply because you fear missing out on an opportunity?

Accept that many opportunities *seem* promising, but are a waste of time and energy. You probably know this from experience. When your inner opportunist rears its head, have the courage to say no, even if doing so means you might miss out.

It'll be difficult in the beginning, especially if you struggle with FOMO. But rest assured, it gets easier with time and consistent application. And once you successfully curb your fear of missing out, you'll find it easier to decline requests that threaten to stretch you too thin.

BONUS STRATEGY #4: SAY NO BY CATEGORY

～

D o you receive the same type of requests on a regular basis? When you're approached with them, is your first inclination to decline? If so, this strategy will save you a significant amount of time. It'll also prevent the requestor from becoming angry because your refusal to help won't be taken as a personal rejection.

Here's how it works:

Suppose you're regularly asked by coworkers to help with accounting-related projects. Such projects lie outside the scope of your job responsibilities. But your coworkers know that you majored in accounting in college, and therefore you're considered a knowledgable resource.

The problem is, you're approached for help so often

that accommodating these requests is preventing you from attending to your own responsibilities.

One solution is to decide that you'll no longer assist your coworkers on accounting-related tasks. You decide to turn down this entire category of requests. Over time, your coworkers will become informed of your decision, and begin to look elsewhere for help.

This strategy isn't just effective for the workplace. It can work in your personal life, too. It did for me.

Recall the section *My Past Life As A People Pleaser*. You may remember that, during my college years, I was the go-to person for helping people move. I owned a pickup truck, and was inclined to say yes to every request. Those two factors made me a perfect candidate for the job.

At a certain point, however, I became resentful. I began to feel that I was being taken for granted. So I stopped accepting "invitations" to help people move. When asked to help, I simply replied, *"I don't help people move anymore."*

It didn't take long for people to stop asking me. And importantly, I didn't lose any true friends. Nor did I become the subject of disdain or ridicule. I simply stopped receiving this type of request.

You can also reject requests during certain times of the day. Returning to our previous example, suppose you're willing to continue helping your coworkers on accounting-related projects. But you decide to turn down any request that requires your attention between 9:00 a.m. and 12:00 noon, your most productive hours.

Or you may decide to turn down all requests that

require more than 30 minutes of your time during the workweek. For example, you're willing to help a friend pack up a few boxes in preparation for a move. But you're *unwilling* to transport the boxes to his or her new residence, which is located two hours away.

When you begin turning down requests based on a particular attribute, you reset others' expectations of you. Your coworkers, friends, and family members will eventually realize that you always decline such requests, and they'll stop seeking for your participation.

This strategy also streamlines the process of saying no. You no longer have to consider each request individually. If it matches your deal-breaking attribute (e.g. the request will require more than 30 minutes of your time), you automatically turn it down.

Those who ask for your time, attention, money, or labor, can't reasonably assume your decision is a personal rejection. After all, you're rejecting the type of request, not the requestor.

Think about the requests you regularly receive, whether at home or at your workplace. If they're weighing you down and taking up too much of your time, try to categorize the worst offenders. Then, decide to reject the entire category.

You may be surprised at how easy it is to say no without feeling guilty using this approach.

YOU'RE NOT RESPONSIBLE FOR OTHERS' REACTIONS

~

One of the biggest stumbling blocks for people pleasers to overcome is feeling responsible for others' feelings. They fear that saying no will disappoint and anger requestors. This fear prompts them to regularly put others' priorities ahead of their own.

This tendency can spring from a number of factors. For example, the individual may desperately want to be liked by other people. He or she may seek validation from others, and saying yes is the easiest path to that end. Or the people pleaser may possess a low self-image, and believe others' happiness is more important than his or her own.

So he or she says yes, even when saying no is clearly a better option.

If you want to learn to say no with confidence and

without guilt, it's vital that you set emotional boundaries. You must avoid feeling responsible for others' feelings, and absolve yourself as the cause of their negative reactions.

As long as you turn down a request with grace and respect, you shouldn't feel accountable if the requestor reacts poorly. You're not the cause of that individual's distress and ire, even if he or she attempts to convince you otherwise. These emotions are borne of circumstances that are outside your control.

For example, the requestor may be having a terrible day, and your refusal to help is the linchpin that sets him or her off. Or the requestor may be experiencing extreme stress due to poor planning on his or her part. Or the requestor might have had an argument with his or her significant other, and the emotions stemming from that interaction end up spilling over to this one.

Ultimately, you're not in control of other people's emotions, and thus cannot be culpable for their reactions.

It goes without saying that intentionally hurting someone is a different matter altogether. If you're rude or disrespectful, expect a negative, and perhaps even a hostile, response. Incivility breeds incivility.

But if you remain courteous, candid, and sincere when turning down requests, and the requestor responds in a hostile manner, let it go. The negative feelings prompting the belligerence come from a place inside him or her over which you have no jurisdiction.

YOUR TIME AND INTERESTS ARE VALUABLE

∼

People pleasers often prioritize others' needs ahead of their own because they feel their time, interests, opinions, and goals are worth less. I know this from experience. It's how I used to think.

This is a self-image problem.

A person who struggles with a low self-image assumes other people are more important than he or she. Consequently, this individual lacks the confidence to act in self-interest. And *that* makes it difficult for him or her to say no.

It's critical that you recognize your own value. This isn't just a matter of building self-esteem. Recognizing your value puts you on an equal footing with everyone around you. To that end, it forces you to acknowledge that your time, interests, opinions, and goals are worth just as much as other people's.

Once you accept this circumstance as truth, you'll find it becomes easier to turn down requests without feeling pangs of guilt. And importantly, you'll be able to do so without wondering whether your decisions earn the requestors' approval.

When you possess a strong sense of self-worth, you naturally feel more confident. And that can give you the courage to stand your ground when you face emotional manipulation or intimidation.

SAYING NO DOESN'T MAKE YOU A BAD PERSON

~

Have you ever wondered why you feel guilty after saying no to someone? It's not because you're a bad person. It's not because you've done something wrong or transgressed against the requestor.

It's a learned response, one that's ingrained in our minds through a lifetime of indoctrination.

Think back to when you were a child. Do you remember how easy it was to say no? You weren't worried about others' feelings. Nor did you concern yourself with matters of etiquette. If you didn't want to do something, you said so. And you didn't beat around the bush or scramble to come up with excuses. You responded with a simple, unequivocal "no."

Fast forward a few years. You're in grade school, and

have discovered that people in authority (your teacher, your parents, etc.) dislike hearing you say no. And you begin hearing feedback to that effect.

The indoctrination has begun in earnest.

Fast forward again, this time to high school. You've received so much negative feedback over the years as the result of saying no that you now hesitate before doing so. You second guess your decisions to turn down requests because you fear offending or angering people. And more often than not, you end up saying yes just to avoid that outcome.

Let's jump forward several more years. You're now focused on your career. By this point, you've endured a lifetime of feedback admonishing you for selfishness, stinginess, and an unwillingness to help. You've been told repeatedly that turning down requests for help is rude and disrespectful. This longstanding feedback has trained you to think that every "no" is worthy of suspicion.

It's no wonder so many of us enter adulthood with the belief that saying no to others makes us bad people!

In reality, depending on your circumstances, saying no may be more appropriate than saying yes. For example, suppose you've made plans to have lunch with a friend. A coworker stops by your office and asks you to help her with a project. The problem is, helping her would require you to cancel - or at least postpone - your lunch date.

In this scenario, turning down your coworker doesn't make you a bad person. In fact, doing so is appropriate as it allows you to fulfill an earlier commitment.

Will people occasionally be disappointed, or even angered, by your refusal to help them? Of course. But remember, you can't control others' reactions. All you can be reasonably expected to do is say no with poise and sincerity.

Remember, it's not your job to appease the requestor. Moreover, refusing to put his or her priorities ahead of your own doesn't make you a disagreeable person. It makes you conscious of competing interests and obligations, and encourages you to manage them sensibly given your limited availability.

START WITH THE SMALL NO'S

~

L earning to say no with confidence is like adopting any new habit. It's best to start small. Take advantage of "easy wins" in the beginning, and grow accustomed to trusting your own convictions. You'll slowly strengthen your sense of personal authority.

How do you start with small no's? Keep your eyes open for opportunities at retail stores. For example, the clerk at a clothing store might ask you to sign up for a store credit account, and save 15% in the process. Politely decline, even if you're tempted by the promised savings.

Suppose you're in line at Starbucks and the barista asks whether you'd like a croissant with your coffee. Say no, even if you begin salivating at the thought.

Retail employees are accustomed to hearing "no."

They hear it hundreds of times each day. They won't be disappointed, angered, or offended if you decline their invitations. Meanwhile, you'll receive free "training" in becoming more assertive.

Next, look for opportunities to say no to people on the phone. For example, suppose someone cold calls you and tries to sell you a timeshare. Respectfully decline the offer. If he or she persists, reiterate your decision and inform the salesperson that you intend to hang up the phone.

Suppose you receive a phone call, and the caller asks you to participate in a survey. This is another chance for you to practice being assertive. Tell the caller no, thank him or her for the call, bid him or her good night, and hang up.

Learning to say no in these "low risk" situations allows you to slowly build your confidence. You can cautiously graduate to steadily higher-risk scenarios as your confidence grows. This approach allows the habit to become entrenched in your mind. The stronger your confidence and faith in your convictions, the easier you'll find saying no to people - even when they become angry, persistent, and emotionally manipulative.

Coming Up Next...

We've covered a variety of practical strategies you can use to turn down requests and decline invitations without feeling guilty. These strategies will also help discourage requestors from taking your refusal to help as a personal rejection.

In *Part IV: How To Say No In Any Situation*, we'll take a closer look at specific scenarios involving the various people in your life. We'll discuss how to say no to your family, friends, neighbors, bosses, and more, and inspire their respect in the process.

PART IV

BONUS SECTION

HOW TO SAY NO IN ANY SITUATION

~

The ability to say no with respect and finesse is one of the most important and rewarding skills you can develop. But it's sometimes difficult to say no to certain people in our lives.

You may have no trouble declining requests from your coworkers, but immediately give in when approached by members of your family.

You might be able to say no to your neighbors without the tiniest twinge of guilt, but find it incredibly difficult to rebuff your friends.

Or perhaps its your clients you're inclined to accommodate against your better judgement. Maybe it's your boss. Or maybe it's random strangers you feel compelled to help.

This section will cover these and other interactions, and teach you how to say no when doing so is in your best interests.

HOW TO SAY NO TO YOUR EXTENDED FAMILY

~

Extended family members can be tough negotiators. When they want something from you (your time, labor, money, etc.), they're often willing to go to great lengths to get you to surrender. I'll bet you can think of at least one relative who's irritatingly persistent and not above using emotional manipulation and bullying to achieve his or her ends.

Saying no to extended family can be uncomfortable. They have higher expectations of you than your coworkers, friends, and neighbors. They *expect* you to drop what you're doing to help them.

This expectation stems from years of training.

Think of a cousin, aunt or uncle, or grandparent who refuses to take no for an answer. She persists when you turn her down. She reacts with anger. She makes you feel guilty for her predicament.

Can you picture this individual? Now, consider whether you've ever given in to her (or him). Have you ever initially said no to her, but ultimately capitulated in frustration? Do you regularly do so when she requests something of you?

If so, you've trained this family member to wear you down. She knows you'll eventually say yes if she's persistent. She knows you'll give in if she can make you feel badly about turning her down.

The solution is to set new expectations. You must establish boundaries that are respected by your relatives.

One method is to create rules regarding what you're willing to help with and what you're *not* willing to help with. For example, does your cousin regularly ask you to run errands for him? If so, create a "no errands" rule. Does your uncle frequently ask you to help him fix his vehicle? If so, create a "no auto repair" rule.

Another tactic is to create rules concerning *when* you'll help. For example, decree that you'll be available to help your relatives on Saturday afternoons. The rest of the week is reserved for you, your spouse, and children.

You can also force persistent and manipulative relatives to leave messages. For example, when they call you for help, let their calls roll to voicemail. When they email you, let some time pass before you reply. When they text you, resist the temptation to respond immediately.

This tactic discourages urgent requests. For example, if your cousin knows that it takes you a few days to return his calls or emails, he'll be less likely to approach you with requests that demand immediate action.

These measures are designed to reset your extended family's expectations of you. Your relatives might be offended in the beginning. They may even show signs of hostility. But with time and consistency, they'll learn that you're not the pushover they've come to expect.

HOW TO SAY NO TO YOUR SPOUSE

~

If you always say yes to your spouse or partner, saying no can seem a bit like tiptoeing through a minefield. Turning down a request can lead to conflict, which, if you and your partner allow it, can quickly spiral out of control.

As adults in loving relationships, we learn through experience that saying yes is, in many ways, an expression of our love, trust, and acceptance of the requestor. But does that mean we should *always* say yes?

Since you've made it this far in *The Art Of Saying NO*, you probably know my answer. Saying no to our partners is not only sometimes necessary, but can add value to our relationships.

Let me explain.

One of the preconditions to a healthy relationship, whether it's one we share with our friends, coworkers, or relatives, is the existence of well-defined boundaries.

A lot of folks think of personal boundaries as a way to keep others at bay. That's reasonable. But boundaries have greater value in the context of your relationship with our spouses or partners.

Boundaries help us to better understand our loved ones. They encourage us to see our spouses and partners as unique individuals with unique feelings, passions, and interests. They make it easier to identify our loved ones' needs. To that end, they discourage us from using guilt or manipulation to get what we desire.

This notion of personal boundaries works in both directions. When you set boundaries with your significant other, you convey your individuality, dislikes, opinions, and personal convictions. Maintaining these boundaries - that is, acting in accordance with your convictions - inspires respect.

Respect lessens the urge to use emotional bullying or manipulation. When you say no, your spouse or partner won't consider your response arbitrary. He or she will be inclined to assume your decision is well-reasoned, and accept it at face value.

Given the above, the first step toward learning to say no to your spouse is to identify your dislikes, opinions, and convictions. Then, establish boundaries that reflect them.

For example, suppose you dislike working on cars. Set a boundary that highlights this aversion. Now let's say your spouse ask you to take a look at her car because it's making a strange sound. You can respond:

66 As you know, I hate working on cars. But I'll be happy to take it to the shop for you."

Or suppose you dislike loud, raucous concerts. It hurts your ears and you're concerned about your safety. Let's say your spouse asks you to accompany him to a heavy metal concert. You can respond:

66 Thanks for asking me. But I'd rather not go. I don't enjoy those types of concerts."

Saying no to your spouse or partner in situations where you harbor strong opinions is empowering. Moreover, when you act according to your convictions, you strengthen the mutual bond of respect that connects the two of you.

HOW TO SAY NO TO YOUR CHILDREN

∽

I t's difficult to say no to kids. As their parent, you want them to be happy and feel fulfilled. You also want to give them the opportunity to experience new things. So, you end up saying yes more often than you think you should.

External pressures also play a role. We don't want our friends and family members to think we're overly strict. And in public, we don't want onlookers and passersby to think of us as uncompromising tyrants. So, we say yes when we'd rather say no.

Meanwhile, children quickly learn what they can get away with. Many intuit that the right amount of emotional manipulation applied at the right time can change a "no" to a "yes." Some children learn to use that to their advantage.

Here's an example:

Child: "Can I spend the night at Sarah's?"
Parent: "No."
Child: "You never let me do anything fun! Sometimes, you make me so angry I could scream!"
Parent: "Fine. Don't throw a tantrum. You can spend the night at Sarah's."

Giving in teaches the child that when you say no, it's not the final word. He or she may be able to persuade you to change your mind. And once that becomes a possibility, expect your child to become persistent and calculating to that end.

Saying no to kids is about setting clear boundaries. It's about articulating what you'll allow them to do and what you won't allow them to do, and setting their expectations accordingly.

Children have a tendency to test the rigidity of their parents' rules. Until they learn otherwise, a simple "no" is actually a "maybe." They presume there's a chance their parents will capitulate.

If you want to assert your parental authority, and have your children accept your decisions, you must be willing to disappoint them. Their agendas will often contradict your own. The key is teaching them that you'll stand your ground once you've made a decision. A "no" will remain a "no" regardless of the tactics they employ in an attempt to change your mind.

Negotiating An Early "No"

Many parents get caught in the negotiation trap.

Some types of negotiation are fair and worth considering. For example, a child might ask, "*If I finish my chores, complete my homework, and take the dog for a walk, can I spend the night at Sarah's?*" This negotiating tactic shows the child understands the positive effect of meeting her responsibilities.

Other types of negotiation are unfair and should immediately be dismissed. For example, this same child might say, "*If you don't let me spend the night at Sarah's, I'm not going to do my chores.*" This is nothing more than a threat.

If you're receptive to negotiation, it's important that you only entertain positive arrangements. For example, agreeing to let your child stay at a friend's house overnight if she completes her chores and homework, and meets her other obligations is a positive approach. It encourages integrity and good character, and at the same time discourages impulsiveness.

On the other hand, surrendering to your child's threat of poor behavior undermines your parental authority. That promises to make saying no increasingly problematic down the road.

Bottom line: saying no to your kids is a matter of setting expectations and standing your ground. Once your kids realize that "no" really means "no," you'll face less manipulative behavior.

HOW TO SAY NO TO YOUR FRIENDS

~

F riends do favors for each other. In fact, they *expect* favors from each other. That's the reason it's diffi-cult to turn down friends' requests. Doing so can lead to more than just disappointment. It can literally cause a friendship to fall apart.

Again, it's mostly a matter of expectations. If a friend expects you to say yes, hearing you say no will likely be confusing and vexing.

In some cases, the expectation may be so deeply rooted in your friend's mind that your circumstances won't matter. Your friend will focus almost entirely on your refusal to help.

Here's how such a conversation might play out:

Friend: "Hey, can you take me to the airport this afternoon?"

You: "No, I don't have time today."

Friend (upset): "Are you serious? I'd help you if you asked me."

You: "And I'd be happy to help if I had the time. But today's not good for me."

Friend (angry): "That's really rude! Don't come to me the next time you need help!"

Failing to meet your friend's expectations can erode the friendship. It can impair the trust and intimacy you share with him or her, and make future conversations tense and even combative.

So, how can you turn down friends without causing offense? How can you say no to them without causing irrevocable harm to your friendships?

First, realize that you owe it to yourself to make time for your own responsibilities and interests. No one will respect your time more than you. So you must remain vigilant, reminding yourself that saying yes to one thing requires saying no to something else. Being a good friend doesn't obligate you to put your friends' priorities ahead of your own.

Second, don't wait until you're frustrated with your friend to say no. Don't consent to request after request, becoming increasingly bitter and resentful that you're being taken for granted, and then proclaim "NO!" in a rage.

Third, remind yourself that your friend's dismay and anger upon hearing you say no isn't your problem. As long as you turn him or her down graciously, sincerely, and with respect, you've done your part.

Fourth, start setting boundaries. If you have a friend who typically reacts poorly when you say no, take him or her aside and discuss the matter. Inform him or her of your feelings, limits, and personal convictions. Be honest with him or her. Explain how catering to others' needs before your own, particularly given your workload and personal responsibilities, is exhausting and upsetting to you.

A true friend will understand your misgivings and respect your boundaries.

Encourage your friends to come to you in the future when they need help. After all, helping friends strengthens the trust and rapport you share with them. It's deeply rewarding to help friends in their times of need.

But make clear that you won't always be able to say yes. There will be times that you'll have to say no. But when you do so, it's always for good reasons - reasons you expect your friends to acknowledge and respect.

HOW TO SAY NO TO YOUR NEIGHBORS

～

Neighbors pose a unique challenge. They're not family, so you're unlikely to feel a lifelong allegiance to them. However, you live near them, so you probably see them on a regular basis - perhaps every day. The last thing you want is for things to be uncomfortable between them and you.

What's a people pleaser to do, particularly if your neighbors are pushy and demanding?

I've heard horror stories of people entering their neighbors' garages uninvited to borrow tools. Some even have the audacity to enter their neighbors' residences.

My brother has a neighbor who'll come over and knock on his door until it's answered. He'll sometimes persist for 20 minutes or more. Worse, he'll look through the mail slot to see if my brother's family is home, and even try the doorknob (presumably to enter if it's not locked).

Hopefully, you're not dealing with these types of neighbors. But even with lesser offenders, it's important to set clear boundaries. These boundaries will make it easier to say no when your neighbors' requests fail to suit you. And importantly, you'll be able to say no without damaging your neighborly relations because your boundaries will already be established.

For example, let's say you work from home. As a result, some of your neighbors - the ones who work all day - ask you to check in on their pets, feeding them and taking them for walks.

This understandably bothers you. You feel taken for granted, especially since working from home doesn't necessarily increase your availability.

So, you decide to set a boundary. Each time a neighbor asks you to care for his or her pet, you explain that you simply don't do that anymore. With time, word will spread that you're unwilling to be your neighbors' pets' caretaker. Reasonable neighbors will respect your decision.

Now, suppose one of your neighbors walks over to your house and tells you that he's going to be away on a week-long vacation. He asks you to feed his dog and take him for a few walks a day. You can respond by saying:

    ““ Jack, you know I don't watch other people's pets anymore. I made that decision so I could focus on my own projects."

"Jack" might be upset. He might become hostile, and even verbally abusive. But remember, negative reactions to your refusal to help have nothing to do with you. In this case, they reflect Jack's unfair expectations.

Saying no to your neighbors will probably feel awkward if you've never done it in the past. That's to be expected. After all, you don't want to offend your neighbors by turning them down.

At the same time, you shouldn't feel guilty putting your priorities ahead of theirs. You're in charge of your time, energy, money, and labor. It's important that you use these limited resources judiciously to care for yourself and those in your charge. You're the only one who can be relied upon to do it.

Proactively set clear boundaries with your neighbors. Then, stick to them with grace and poise. Over time, you'll become increasingly comfortable with saying no, which will help to align your neighbors' expectations with your own convictions.

HOW TO SAY NO TO YOUR COWORKERS

~

The workplace can sometimes seem like a battlefield of competing interests and conflicting agendas. You'll inevitably be approached by coworkers, and asked to help on a variety of tasks and pet projects.

The problem is, you have your own work-related responsibilities and limited time and energy with which to work on them.

In this environment, it pays to know how to say no with assertiveness.

You'll find that many of the strategies covered in *Part III: 10 Strategies For Saying No (Without Feeling Like A Jerk)* are especially effective in the workplace. For example, asking requestors to follow up at a later time (Strategy #6) is a great way to gauge the urgency of a coworker's request.

Suggesting other coworkers who are more knowledgable and better qualified than you (Strategy #9) benefits you *and* the requestor. The requestor is given a more valuable resource to leverage while you're able to save time and resume your focus on your own work.

Rejecting requests by category (Bonus Strategy #4) gives you a hassle-free way to say no to coworkers. It's consistent with skill specialization in the workplace.

Consider that we spend the majority of our time on tasks and activities that fall into specific categories. These tasks and activities are a part of our specialized skill sets. They improve our productivity and help us to minimize errors and waste. When we're asked by our coworkers to help on projects that lie outside these skill sets, we can reasonably say no.

The manner in which you turn down coworkers' requests is important. Don't make excuses. Don't invent reasons to decline requests. Be genuine and graceful, and own your decision.

For example, suppose a coworker asks for your help on her pet project. You could respond:

> Thanks for asking me, Sharon. I appreciate your confidence in me. But I don't want to break away from my own projects."

Or you can respond:

" I'm unskilled in that area, and therefore won't be much help to you. So I'm going to say no."

There's no need to apologize. Nor is there a need to be evasive. Simply state your intention as clearly as possible. And take ownership of your decision by saying "*I don't*" or "*I won't*" instead of saying "*I can't.*"

You'll find that your coworkers will have more respect for your time if you stop consenting to every request. They'll come to realize you're most likely to accommodate them when you have the availability, and their requests align with your professional needs, personal convictions, and long-term goals.

HOW TO SAY NO TO YOUR BOSS

~

I deally, your boss would be aware of your workload. He or she would know what's on your plate, and have a solid grasp of your availability. So when your boss assigns new projects and delegates new tasks, he or she would reprioritize your current responsibilities.

That's how things *should* work, anyway.

Unfortunately, the real world runs less smoothly. Does the following scenario sound familiar?

You're sitting in your office working through a mile-long to-do list. You're also fielding phone calls from coworkers, clients, and vendors. While you work, a small voice in the back of your head nags you to respond to emails and return phone calls.

You look at the clock and realize you have a meeting in

15 minutes. It's one of many scheduled throughout the day. You silently think, *"how can I get anything accomplished with so many meetings on my calendar?"*

At that moment, you glance at the inbox on your desk. You instantly regret doing so. Despite your best efforts, your inbox is growing, making you feel as if you've yet to make a serious dent in your workload.

You feel your stress levels rising. You have too much to do and not enough time to get everything done. Worse, there's no light at the end of the tunnel.

While you're feeling overwhelmed, you receive an email from your boss. Curious, you click to read it. She's asking you to take on yet another project. You sigh in discouragement because you have neither the time nor bandwidth. You barely have time to take a lunch break.

But how do you say no? How do you turn down your boss, the person who controls your professional time?

Many folks simply absorb the new work. They grin and bear it because they feel uncomfortable saying no. They fear their bosses will consider them difficult to work with, which might negatively impact their careers.

But there's value in communicating your limits. You'll not only manage your stress levels, but you'll also avoid being stretched too thin. The last thing you want is to take on new projects for which you have no time. Doing so is a recipe for frustration and failure.

While saying no may be difficult - delivering bad news is *always* difficult - there are ways you can soften the blow. Following are a few suggestions.

First, when responding to your boss, be forthright about your current workload and resulting lack of availability. Explain that you wouldn't be able to do a good job on the new project given everything else that's on your plate. If you're already working under pending deadlines, mention them.

Second, ask questions regarding the new project. When is it due? What does it involve? What skills are required? Will you need to coordinate activities among a group of participants?

Third, ask your boss to reprioritize your workload. Suggest postponing an existing project that's on your plate so you can devote your time and attention to the new project.

Fourth, if none of your current projects and tasks can be rescheduled, ask whether the *new* project can be postponed. For example, you might tell your boss that you'll have more bandwidth in five days, after you've completed your current deliverables.

You can say no to your boss without actually using the word "no." In fact, doing so is a smart tactic since "no" carries a negative connotation. The more important point is that you communicate your limitations and offer alternative solutions that'll help your boss accomplish what he or she wants.

HOW TO SAY NO TO YOUR CLIENTS

~

Some clients are a dream to work with. They're communicative regarding their needs, set reasonable time frames for deliverables, and are willing to allow you, the person they've hired, to work according to your process. Moreover, they pay your invoices in a timely manner.

And then there are the difficult clients. These clients insist you meet unreasonable deadlines. They regularly demand that you perform duties that lie outside the terms of your contract or agreement. And they micromanage your work to the point that you dread working on the projects for which they've hired you.

It's relatively easy to say no to the latter group. Turning down projects from clients who are disrespectful and overly demanding is a matter of survival. They take up too much time while delivering too little compensation for the effort and aggravation.

But even great clients sometimes make requests you're better off turning down. For example, you may lack the resources to take on a certain project. If you were to consent to the project, you'd be setting yourself up for failure. Or perhaps the time and effort required are too great given the compensation. Or maybe it's a good project, but you've planned a vacation that limits your availability.

The point is, there are often valid reasons to say no to clients, even the ones you enjoy working with. But doing so can still be difficult. You don't want to disappoint them or hurt their feelings. You don't want to hurt the relationship. And you certainly don't want to lose their business.

So how can you say no to clients in a way that'll ensure they respect your decisions?

First, recognize that turning down a client's project isn't a negative reflection of your service or professionalism. On the contrary, it shows that you know your limits and have a solid sense regarding how you want to run your business.

Second, provide a legitimate reason for declining the request. For example, you might say:

> I'm going to pass on this project because I don't have the resources (or skills) to do a good job for you."

Or you could explain:

❝ I'll be on vacation next month, so I won't have time to work on this for you."

Reasons validate your decisions. A client who understands why you're turning down her request is more likely to forgive you for doing so.

Third, offer an alternative. For example, if your lack of availability is preventing you from taking on a project, suggest a deadline that's further down the road. Or if you lack the skill set required to complete the project, refer your client to someone you trust who possesses the necessary skills. If you're simply not interested in the project, suggest a qualified peer who might be willing to take it on in your stead.

Saying no to clients is rarely fun. That's especially true if you genuinely like them and enjoy working with them. But depending on your circumstances, saying no is sometimes your best option. As long as you're communicative, candid, and respectful, you can do so without harming the relationship. As a bonus, you'll be setting the expectation that you will occasionally say no.

HOW TO SAY NO TO STRANGERS

∾

For some of us, saying no to strangers is easy. We don't feel a personal connection to them. Nor do we feel a sense of allegiance or obligation. So when we're faced with a stranger's request, one we'd prefer to decline, it's easy to do so.

For others, turning down strangers is nearly as difficult as turning down friends and family members. Refusing to help someone, even a person they don't know, causes them to feel guilty.

If you fall into the second camp, and want to learn to say no to strangers without guilt, I recommend doing the following three things.

First, think about where your obligations begin and end when it comes to strangers. This self-analysis should take into account your values and convictions. Note that this is a personal matter. You'll inevitably feel differently than other people.

For example, many people feel obligated to give money to panhandlers. Others believe that doing so is morally questionable. Your ability to say no to panhandlers will depend, in part, on where you stand on the matter.

The goal isn't to conform to others' standards. Remember, you don't need other people's approval. Rather, the goal is for you to identify *your* standards, and align your decisions so they're consistent with them. If you feel it's wrong to give money to panhandlers, you'll find it easier to say no since refusing is in harmony with your convictions.

Second, don't be afraid to say you're uncomfortable with a stranger's request. For example, suppose you're relaxing at a park. A stranger approaches you and asks you to watch his dog for 30 minutes while he runs an errand. You can say:

> 66 I don't know you or your dog. I'm uncomfortable watching him because doing so makes me liable if he bites someone."

Third, employ *Bonus Strategy #4: Say No By Category*. Create a rule that precludes participating in certain activities. If a stranger asks you for help, and your consent would violate this rule, say no and state your reason.

For example, let's say you've stopped by Starbucks for a cup of coffee. You're leaving the venue and heading for your vehicle when you're stopped by a stranger. He asks you to give him a ride to the train station. Saying no is easy if you've decided beforehand to reject all such requests. You can respond:

> I have a rule that I don't give rides to strangers."

That is all that's required. If the requestor tries to convince you to consent (e.g. *"C'mon, I'm a trustworthy guy!"*), simply refer again to your rule and stick to your decision.

None of the above is to suggest that you should avoid helping strangers. To be sure, there's joy in doing nice things for people who are unfamiliar to us. But for reasons related to your safety, personal convictions, or lack of resources, saying no is often the better response.

HOW TO SAY NO TO YOURSELF

∾

At any given time, we're subject to temptations that threaten to consume our time, money, labor, and other resources. Such temptations usually distract us from our goals. Being able to resist them - essentially, saying no to ourselves - is key to living a healthy, rewarding life.

For example, let's say you're trying to shed a few pounds. You've decided to stay away from junk food to help you accomplish that goal. Unaware that you've forbidden yourself to eat junk food, a coworker brings donuts to the office.

You have two choices:

1. say no to yourself and remain committed to your goal
2. give in to temptation and chow down

Or suppose you have a long list of chores to do that's likely to take the majority of the day. You need to vacuum and dust the house, wash several loads of laundry, and clean the kitchen and bathrooms. But out of the blue, a friend calls and invites you to spend the day lounging at his or her house.

Once again, your choices are clear:

1. say no to yourself and remain committed to completing your chores
2. surrender to temptation and abandon your chores

Resisting temptations is crucial to staying focused on, and committed to, our goals. The question is, how can we do it effectively? How can we say no to ourselves when we want to give in and say yes?

Here's a solution that works for me: make "I don't" statements. These statements are a declaration of what you choose not to do.

For example, when you're offered a donut, you might say, *"I don't eat donuts."* If you're invited to a friend's house, and have chores looming, you could say, *"I don't like leaving chores undone. Can we get together tomorrow?"*

Think of the various temptations you might encounter,

and how making an "I don't" statement can help you to say no. Here are a few examples:

Temptation: skip your daily visit to the gym.
"I don't" response: *"I don't skip visits to the gym."*

Temptation: make a frivolous, expensive purchase.
"I don't" response: *"I don't spend money frivolously."*

Temptation: gossip about a coworker.
"I don't" response: *"I don't gossip."*

Temptation: binge-watch Netflix when you should be working.
"I don't" response: *"I don't dawdle when there's work to be done."*

When you give in to temptations, you become a slave to your impulses. The resulting short-term gratification often comes at the expense of long-term fulfillment.

When you *resist* temptations with declarative statements that begin with *"I don't…"* you become the architect of a life built upon healthy intentions.

FINAL THOUGHTS ON THE ART OF SAYING NO

∼

I t's important to remember the effects of saying *yes*. When you consent to other people's requests and put their priorities ahead of your own, you give up control of precious resources - most notably your time. Once these resources are squandered, they cannot be reclaimed.

We tend to presume that most requests will only require a small commitment from us. But too often, that's untrue. A request that's promised to take "a couple of minutes" ends up taking half an hour. A favor that's promised to take an hour ends up consuming half the day.

Moreover, the cumulative demand of numerous small requests can be substantial. Saying yes to multiple people can easily swallow your most productive hours.

Throughout *The Art Of Saying NO*, I've shown you how to turn down requests, invitations, favors, and anything else that invades your boundaries without feeling guilty. The strategies we've covered will also mitigate the requestor's disappointment at hearing the word "no."

But that doesn't mean saying no will be easy - at least, not in the beginning. Doing so with confidence is like using a muscle. You need to *use* a muscle to make it stronger.

So, I encourage you to put the strategies in *The Art Of Saying NO* to immediate use. Start small with low-risk situations - for example, telling your server at a restaurant that *"No. I don't want dessert. Thanks."* Then gradually use the strategies in higher-risk situations.

With time and application, you'll find yourself becoming more assertive. Saying no will become easier as you learn to rely on your convictions. As a bonus, you'll find that your friends, family members, coworkers, and neighbors will become more respectful of your time and decisions.

DID YOU ENJOY READING THE ART OF SAYING NO?

~

Thanks so much for reading *The Art Of Saying NO*. I realize there are many other ways you could've spent your time. I'm honored that you spent some of it with me.

If you enjoyed reading *The Art Of Saying NO*, would you do me a small favor? Would you leave a short review for the book at Amazon? A sentence or two about something you liked would mean the world to me. Most importantly, your comments will encourage other folks to give the book a try.

One last thing before we part ways (for now). I plan to write several books over the next twelve months. I'll be releasing each of them at a steep discount; you'll be able to grab each one for less than $1.

If you'd like to be notified when these books are released, and take advantage of the discount pricing, be sure to join my mailing list. You'll receive my 40-page PDF ebook titled *Catapult Your Productivity! The Top 10 Habits You Must Develop To Get More Things Done.*

You can join my list at the following address:

http://artofproductivity.com/free-gift/

I'll also send you my best productivity and time management tips via my email newsletter. You'll receive tips and tactics on beating procrastination, creating morning routines, avoiding burnout, developing razor-sharp focus, along with many other productivity hacks!

If you have questions or would like to share a productivity tip that has made a difference in your life, please feel free to reach out to me at damon@artofproductivity.com. I'd love to hear about it!

Until next time,

Damon Zahariades
http://artofproductivity.com

ABOUT THE AUTHOR

Damon Zahariades is a corporate refugee who endured years of unnecessary meetings, drive-by chats with coworkers, and a distraction-laden work environment before striking out on his own. Today, in addition to being the author of a growing catalog of time management and productivity books, he's the showrunner for the productivity blog ArtofProductivity.com.

In his spare time, he shows off his copywriting chops by powering the content marketing campaigns used by today's growing businesses to attract customers.

Damon lives in Southern California with his beautiful, supportive wife and their frisky dog. He's currently staring down the barrel of his 50th birthday.

OTHER BOOKS BY DAMON ZAHARIADES

The Joy Of Imperfection: A Stress-Free Guide To Silencing Your Inner Critic, Conquering Perfectionism, and Becoming The Best Version Of Yourself!

Is perfectionism causing you to feel stressed, irritated, and chronically unhappy? Here's how to silence your inner critic, embrace imperfection, and live without fear!

∼

The Procrastination Cure: 21 Proven Tactics For Conquering Your Inner Procrastinator, Mastering Your Time, And Boosting Your Productivity!

Do you struggle with procrastination? Discover how to take quick action, make fast decisions, and finally overcome your inner procrastinator!

Morning Makeover: How To Boost Your Productivity,

Explode Your Energy, and Create An Extraordinary Life - One Morning At A Time!

Would you like to start each day on the right foot? Here's how to create quality morning routines that set you up for more daily success!

Fast Focus: A Quick-Start Guide To Mastering Your Attention, Ignoring Distractions, And Getting More Done In Less Time!

Are you constantly distracted? Does your mind wander after just a few minutes? Learn how to develop laser-sharp focus!

Small Habits Revolution: 10 Steps To Transforming Your Life Through The Power Of Mini Habits!

Got 5 minutes a day? Use this simple, effective plan for creating any new habit you desire!

To-Do List Formula: A Stress-Free Guide To Creating To-Do Lists That Work!

Finally! A step-by-step system for creating to-do lists that'll actually help you to get things done!

The 30-Day Productivity Plan: Break The 30 Bad Habits That Are Sabotaging Your Time Management - One Day At A Time!

Need a daily action plan to boost your productivity? This 30-day guide is the solution to your time management woes!

The Time Chunking Method: A 10-Step Action Plan For Increasing Your Productivity

It's one of the most popular time management strategies used today. Double your productivity with this easy 10-step system.

Digital Detox: The Ultimate Guide To Beating Technology Addiction, Cultivating Mindfulness, and Enjoying More Creativity, Inspiration, And Balance In Your Life!

Are you addicted to Facebook and Instagram? Are you obsessed with your phone? Use this simple, step-by-step plan to take a technology vacation!

For a complete list, please visit

http://artofproductivity.com/my-books/

Printed in Poland
by Amazon Fulfillment
Poland Sp. z o.o., Wrocław

63375780R00096